PENGUIN CLASSICS

ON LIBERTY

JOHN STUART MILL was born in London in 1806. A child of precocious intelligence, he was systematically educated by his father, James Mill, to follow in his footsteps as champion of the utilitarian philosophy. By the age of twenty he had achieved this aim: he was leader of the younger philosophical radicals, active as a propagandist in their intellectual and reforming pursuits. In 1826, however, he endured his first period of mental crisis and found he no longer believed in many aspects of the Benthamite creed. He then began a systematic examination of the alternative positions offered by Coleridge, Carlyle, the St Simonians, Comte and Tocqueville, while keeping his links with the utilitarian circle and contributing to their journal, the *London and Westminster Review*.

By the 1840s Mill was able to put forward a mature reinterpretation of his philosophical position; his *System of Logic* (1843) and the *Principles of Political Economy* (1848) formed the basis for his dominant position in Victorian intellectual life. During the years 1859–65 he wrote the other works for which he is now famous: *On Liberty*, *Representative Government*, *Utilitarianism*, *Examination of Sir William Hamilton's Philosophy*, and *Auguste Comte and Positivism*.

After working for thirty-five years in the East India Company, Mill was a Member of Parliament from 1865 to 1868, voting with the Radical party and strongly advocating women's suffrage. He was also concerned with such issues as the Irish land question, slavery and the American Civil War, income and property taxation, tenure reform, and trade unionism. He died at Avignon in 1873, having finished his *Autobiography* in the same year.

•

GERTRUDE HIMMELFARB was educated at Brooklyn College and the University of Chicago. She is Professor of History at the City University of New York and a Fellow of the American Academy of Arts and Sciences. A member of the editorial boards of several scholarly journals, she has received fellowships from the American Council of Learned Societies, the National Endowment of the Humanities, and the Rockefeller and Guggenheim Foundations. She is the author of numerous books, including *Victorian Minds*, *Darwin and the Darwinian Revolution*, *Lord Acton: A Study in Conscience and Politics* and *On Liberty and Liberalism: The Case of John Stuart Mill*.

JOHN STUART MILL

On Liberty

EDITED WITH AN INTRODUCTION BY
GERTRUDE HIMMELFARB

PENGUIN BOOKS

Penguin Books Ltd, 27 Wrights Lane, London w8 5tz (Publishing and Editorial)
and Harmondsworth, Middlesex, England (Distribution and Warehouse)
Viking Penguin Inc., 40 West 23rd Street, New York, New York 10010, USA
Penguin Books Australia Ltd, Ringwood, Victoria, Australia
Penguin Books Canada Ltd, 2801 John Street, Markham, Ontario, Canada l3r 1b4
Penguin Books (NZ) Ltd, 182–190 Wairau Road, Auckland 10, New Zealand

First published 1859
Published in Pelican Books 1974
Reprinted 1976, 1977, 1978, 1979, 1980, 1981
Reissued in the Penguin English Library 1982
Reprinted 1983 (twice), 1984, 1985
Reprinted in Penguin Classics 1985, 1986, 1987, 1988

Made and printed in Great Britain by
Richard Clay Ltd, Bungay, Suffolk
Set in Monotype Garamond

Contents

ON LIBERTY

I

In an age which prides itself on its liberation from all absolutes, which has succeeded in making the very word 'absolute' sound archaic, there is one concept that has very nearly the status of an absolute. That is the idea of liberty. However much the idea may be violated in practice, however much it may be distorted in conception, the idea itself continues to exercise that ultimate authority which once belonged to the idea of God, nature, justice, reason, or the ideal polity. Even those régimes which consistently and flagrantly violate the most elementary precepts of liberty feel obliged to pay lip-service to the idea by claiming for themselves another kind of liberty: 'positive' liberty, a 'higher' freedom than 'mere' freedom. And those régimes which are most solicitous of liberty, whose institutions are designed to provide a considerable measure of liberty, are under constant reproach for falling short of the fullest measure of liberty. Indeed it is the most liberal countries that are most vulnerable to the charge of illiberality. There is hardly a matter of public concern that does not, sooner or later, raise the issue of liberty; not casually, peripherally, as one of a number of considerations to be taken into account, but as the basic and decisive consideration. The use and abuse of drugs, crime and punishment, pornography and obscenity, industrial and economic controls, racial and sexual equality, national security and defence, ecology, technology, bureaucracy, education, religion, the family, sex – all come up against the ultimate test: the liberty of the individual. Nor are the most venerable institutions immune to this challenge. It was once only revolutionaries and social rebels who denounced the 'bourgeois' family as authoritarian, ridiculed 'middle-class' notions of sexual normality and morality, declared all social conventions to be incompatible with individuality, and condemned all authorities – the state, the law, the Church, parents and elders – as agents of coercion. Today these

7

opinions are the common coin of most liberals. Inevitably the elevation of the idea of liberty has led to the debasement of the idea of authority. As particular authorities have become suspect, so also has the very idea of authority. Deprived of legitimacy, of any presumption of right, authority is reduced to nothing more than the exercise of power or force.

What we are left with then, is what John Stuart Mill, more than anyone else, bequeathed to us: the idea of the free and sovereign individual. Intellectual bequests, to be sure, are notoriously complicated and devious. The court of public opinion, through which such bequests are probated, is far more erratic than the courts of law. If it is difficult to establish the paternity of an idea, it is still more difficult to assign responsibility for that idea once it is launched upon the world. Yet there must be some responsibility for ideas as there is for wayward children – a moral if not a legal responsibility. The filiation of ideas was once aptly described by Lord Acton: 'Ideas have a radiation and development, an ancestry and posterity of their own, in which men play the part of godfathers and godmothers more than that of legitimate parents.'[1] At the very least it is this role of godfather that can be ascribed to Mill. And godfathers, it may be remembered, in Mill's time as in Acton's, had a more intimate relationship to their godchildren than is common today.

In one sense, of course, liberty had a long and honourable lineage before Mill. Acton himself traced it back to antiquity, indeed found it more prevalent in some periods of antiquity than in some periods of modernity. But in the sense in which it is widely held today, not as one of several principles making for a good life and a sound polity but as the pre-eminent and ultimate principle, it is peculiarly modern. And even within modernity, it is of relatively recent vintage. Milton's *Areopagitica* is often cited as the Magna Carta of free thought. But Milton intended that freedom to apply only to the toleration of 'neighbouring differences, or rather indifferences'; he explicitly excluded such differences as might subvert religious

1. *Letters of Lord Acton to Mary Gladstone*, ed. Herbert Paul, 1st ed.; New York, 1905, p. 99 (15 March 1880).

or civil authority – 'popery and open superstition', or any opinion 'impious or evil absolutely either against faith or manners'.[2] Similarly, Locke seems, at first sight, to posit a liberty strikingly similar to Mill's; the 'perfect freedom' of all men to 'order their actions and dispose of their possessions and persons as they think fit,' on condition only of their obeying the law of nature that 'no one ought to harm another in his life, health, liberty, or possessions'. But that liberty existed, for Locke, only in a state of nature. And it was precisely because that state of nature was inadequate that men entered civil society and consented to limit not only their liberty of action but also of opinion: 'No opinions contrary to human society, or to those moral rules which are necessary to the preservation of civil society, are to be tolerated by the magistrate.' The denial of the existence of God, for example, could not be tolerated, because 'promises, covenants, and oaths, which are the bonds of human society, can have no hold upon the atheist'.[3]

And so it was with Mill's more immediate predecessors and contemporaries: Adam Smith, the Founding Fathers, Paine and Godwin, Emerson and Thoreau, Proudhon and Stirner. Each celebrated liberty in one fashion or another, to one degree or another. But it remained for Mill to convert the idea of liberty into a philosophically respectable doctrine, to put it in its most comprehensive, extensive, and systematic form, the form in which it is generally known and accepted today.

2

Mill brought to the doctrine of liberty not only a single-mindedness of purpose that immediately attracted attention but also an intellectual authority that commanded instant respect. In 1859 when *On Liberty* appeared, he was fifty-three,

2. John Milton, *Prose Writings*, Everyman ed.; London, 1961, p. 182.
3. John Locke, *Two Treatises on Government*, ed. Peter Laslett, Cambridge, 1967, pp. 287, 289; *A Letter Concerning Toleration*, ed. Patrick Romanell, New York, 1955, pp. 50, 52.

the author of numerous essays which had earned him the reputation of a formidable social critic, and of two major works which had established him as the foremost philosopher and economist in England. His contemporaries have eloquently testified to the intellectual power he wielded, especially during the 1850s and '60s. His *System of Logic* was the standard text in Oxford, and his *Principles of Political Economy*, although not required reading, was the gospel of all those who had any intellectual pretensions. The Conservative statesman and philosopher, Lord Balfour, who was neither a disciple of Mill nor much given to exaggeration, said in recalling his own student days at Cambridge: 'Mill possessed an authority in the English Universities ... comparable to that wielded forty years earlier by Hegel in Germany and in the Middle Ages by Aristotle.'[4] Leslie Stephen, a tutor at Cambridge and an admirer of Mill (although not an uncritical one), described Mill's authority in similar terms: 'In our little circle the summary answer to all hesitating proselytes was, "read Mill". In those argumentations of which I have spoken, hour after hour was given to discussing points raised by Mill as keenly as medieval commentators used to discuss the doctrines of Aristotle.'[5]

Mill's credentials, therefore, were impeccable. And not only was he in his own right, by virtue of his own writings, the intellectual *par excellence*. He also held that title by hereditary right, so to speak, having been born and bred in the very centre of the intellectual establishment. In the history of thought, the son has so far outdistanced the father that it is difficult to keep in mind the importance of James Mill and the community of which he was a part. In his own time, James

4. A. J. Balfour, *Theism and Humanism*, London, 1915, p. 138.
5. Leslie Stephen, *Some Early Impressions*, London, 1924, pp. 71, 75. See also Herbert Spencer, *An Autobiography*, London, 1904, vol. II, p. 247; Henry Fawcett, 'His influence at the Universities', in *John Stuart Mill: His Life and Work*, Boston, 1873, pp. 74–5; John Morley, *Oracles on Man and Government*, London, 1923, pp. 4, 238; Morley, *Recollections*, New York, 1917, vol. I, p. 60; James Bryce, *Studies in Contemporary Biography*, London, 1903, p. 93; Henry Adams, *Cycle of Adams Letters*, Boston, 1920, vol. II, p. 96 (23 October 1863). See also footnotes 69, 70, 77 below.

Mill was a figure of considerable intellectual stature, diminished only by the even more commanding figure of his avowed master, Jeremy Bentham, the father of English utilitarianism. Bentham, himself a bachelor, took a great interest in the education of his chief disciple's eldest son, especially since he was at this time engaged in drawing up an ideal course of education for a youth of the 'middling and higher ranks of life'.[6] Although it was the father who supervised his son's daily education (the boy never attended any school or university), there is no doubt that both Bentham and James Mill looked upon the young boy as their heir-designate and that they intended to make of him the complete utilitarian – which is to say, the perfectly rational man.

This experiment in education has been dramatically recounted in John Mill's *Autobiography*. In reading that account it is easy to be distracted by the sheer precocity of the young Mill: the fact that he read Greek by the age of three, had assimilated a considerable body of classical and historical literature before he was eight, and had mastered philosophy, political economy, mathematics, and the like by the ripe age of twelve. If one discounts Mill's modest disclaimer that what he did could have been done by 'any boy or girl of average capacity and healthy physical constitution',[7] one must credit his own estimate of the immense saving in time represented by this intensive course of study; it gave him, he reckoned, a quarter-of-a-century advantage over most of his contemporaries. But more important, it gave him a sustained training in reasoning and analysis. When he was eleven, for example, in addition to

6. Bentham's *Chrestomathia* was first published in 1816 and reprinted in his *Collected Works*, ed. John Bowring, London, 1843, vol. VIII, pp. 1–191. It is curious to find that John Stuart Mill's education differed markedly from the model of the *Chrestomathia*. The latter provided for an extensive study of the natural and physical sciences and dispensed happily with such 'crabbed and repulsive' subjects as the 'dead languages'. Bentham did, however, exempt from his scheme those youths who intended to enter the professions of law, medicine and divinity, where 'classical learning, and other polite accomplishments' were the tools of the trade. (Vol. VIII, p. 17.) Perhaps the young Mill came under this last dispensation.

7. John Stuart Mill, *Autobiography*, ed. John Jacob Coss, Columbia University ed.; New York, 1924, p. 21.

his other studies, he had the task of reading aloud each day a portion of the manuscript of the *History of India* his father was then preparing for publication, the reading being accompanied by an analysis of the society and institutions of India compared with those of England, and by a critique of England as it was, compared with how it ought to be. Two years later his daily assignment was a written abstract of his father's discourses on the subject of political economy; these reports were discussed and rewritten until they satisfied his father, who then used them in preparing his *Elements of Political Economy*. (The work, published in 1821, included paragraph-résumés prepared by the youngster.) It was this kind of training, a training in the use of mind, that was the truly remarkable feature of Mill's education.

Whatever intellectual vicissitudes Mill was later to experience, this part of his education remained with him. But it became, at critical moments of his life, a terrible burden. No less famous than the account of his education was the account, also in the *Autobiography*, of the 'crisis' he went through at the age of twenty, when the whole of his education was, in effect, called into question. The young man was then well on his way to assuming the position for which he had been groomed: he was engaged in the formidable work of preparing the five-volume edition of Bentham's *Rationale of Judicial Evidence* (formidable, because Bentham's peculiar habits of composition made this more a task of organizing and writing than of mere editing); he was a regular contributor to the Benthamite journal, the *Westminster Review*; he had founded and was actively involved in a debating club which he had named the Utilitarian Society (this was the first time 'utilitarian' was used in this sectarian sense) – all this in addition to his full-time job at the East India Office where he worked directly under his father. It was at this point, when his career seemed to be proceeding along the lines that had been laid out for it, that it underwent a sudden reversal. The nervous breakdown he then suffered was 'mental' in both senses of that word, intellectual and emotional.

He later recognized this crisis as a crisis of faith, rather like, he thought, the familiar experience of the Methodist smitten by a 'conviction of sin'.[8] In his case, the crisis took the form of a fateful question:

'Suppose that all your objects in life were realized; that all the changes in institutions and opinions which you are looking forward to, could be completely effected at this very instant: would this be a great joy and happiness to you?' And an irrepressible self-consciousness distinctly answered, 'No!' At this my heart sank within me: the whole foundation on which my life was constructed fell down. All my happiness was to have been found in the continual pursuit of this end. The end had ceased to charm, and how could there ever again be any interest in the means? I seemed to have nothing left to live for.[9]

That irrepressible 'No!' testified at first only to the failure of utilitarianism to provide a satisfactory basis for his own life, the life of the dedicated reformer. But implicit in it was the recognition of a larger inadequacy. The difficulty was not only his inability to find his personal happiness in the 'greatest happiness of the greatest number', as the utilitarian formula had it; it was also in the utilitarian idea of happiness itself – the idea that happiness could be expressed by a calculus of pleasure and pain, a calculus that could only be arrived at rationally, analytically.[10] What depressed him even more than the loss of his sense of vocation was the absence in him of any natural and spontaneous feeling, any poetic and artistic sensibility. He was convinced that the exclusive cultivation of the 'habit of analysis' had destroyed in him all capacity for emotion.[11]

For six months he continued in a near-suicidal state of depression, apathetically going about his ordinary activities,

8. ibid. p. 94.
9. ibid.
10. It was an essential part of the utilitarian philosophy that personal and collective happiness be intimately related. Thus James Mill, in his article on education in the *Encyclopaedia Britannica*, opened with the proposition: 'The end of Education is to render the individual, as much as possible, an instrument of happiness, first to himself, and next to other beings.' (Reprinted, London, 1825, p. 3.)
11. *Autobiography*, p. 96.

confessing his thoughts to no one because he felt no one in his circle would understand them. Suddenly, as he recalled it in his *Autobiography*, a ray of light broke through:

> I was reading, accidentally, Marmontel's *Mémoires,* and came to the passage which relates his father's death, the distressed position of the family, and the sudden inspiration by which he, then a mere boy, felt and made them feel that he would be everything to them – would supply the place of all that they had lost. A vivid conception of the scene and its feelings came over me, and I was moved to tears. From this moment my burthen grew lighter. The oppression of the thought that all feeling was dead within me, was gone. I was no longer hopeless: I was not a stock or a stone.[12]

A generation raised on Freud will have no difficulty in interpreting this episode, and may only wonder at Mill's innocence in so blandly recounting it. Eight years later, during his father's final, prolonged illness, Mill suffered another breakdown, clearly as much 'mental' as physical, which he neglected to mention in his *Autobiography*.[13] The early fictional fantasy of his father's death was obviously easier to confront than the later reality. But if Mill was unaware of this dimension of the first crisis, he was sufficiently aware of its implications at another level. He was conscious of being liberated from a philosophy that had very nearly killed him, that had rendered him as lifeless as 'a stock or a stone'. In his tears, he found visible evidence of feeling, emotion, passion, life itself.

In our own awareness of the psychological depths of this crisis, we may be inclined to pay too little heed to its intellectual substance. Yet it was of the greatest intellectual moment. For it signified a new mode of thought that was to have the largest and most enduring consequences, not only for *On Liberty* but for all of Mill's writings. Mill himself was acutely sensible of this, although he somewhat understated it in his *Autobiography*. Recounting this stage of his 'mental progress', he described it

12. ibid. p. 99.
13. Alexander Bain, *John Stuart Mill*, New York, 1882, p. 42; J. A. Froude, *Thomas Carlyle: A History of his Life in London*, London, 1884, vol. I, p. 74. See also Gertrude Himmelfarb, *Victorian Minds*, London, 1968, p. 125.

as a compromise between the new and the old. In embracing a philosophy of 'anti-self-consciousness', he said he had not discarded whatever remained valid in utilitarianism. He continued to believe that happiness was 'the test of all rules of conduct, and the end of life'. But he now thought it could be attained only if it were not made the direct and conscious end of life, but regarded rather as a by-product of other ends – the happiness of others, the improvement of mankind, art, beauty, the contemplation of nature, any activity pursued for its own sake. The 'internal culture of the individual', which utilitarianism had so fatally ignored, was one of the 'prime necessities of human well-being', of happiness itself. Mill hastened to add that he did not at this time renounce 'intellectual culture', the role of analysis either in the life of the individual or for the reform of society. He only meant to supplement that intellectual culture by an internal culture, to make the 'cultivation of the feelings' as primary as the cultivation of reason. In the private realm this meant giving a far greater emphasis to poetry, art, music, nature, whatever would stimulate the individual's sensibilities and passions. In the public realm it meant giving far less importance to the 'ordering of outward circumstances'. Social relations, he realized, were much more complicated than the Benthamites had assumed; politics was not a science, there was no one set of model institutions, and there was a large and important area of life which did not and should not come within the purview of the legislator or reformer.[14]

Mill was to go through several other 'periods', as he described them, in the course of his personal and intellectual history.[15] But this initial crisis of faith remained the decisive experience of his life and was reflected, in one way or another, in each of his major works. In his *Autobiography* he remarked upon the fact that he was inspired to rethink his early – that is, his father's – views on logic, and ultimately to write his own *System of Logic*, as a result of the recognition forced upon him at this time that his father's philosophic method was fundamen-

14. *Autobiography*, pp. 100–101.
15. ibid. pp. 129, 133.

tally erroneous in matters of politics and morals. One might well say the same of *On Liberty*, large parts of which read as if they had been written under the direct inspiration or the most vivid memory of this crisis. Indeed the original sketch of *On Liberty* was written at the same time that he was working on his autobiographical account of the crisis, and he rewrote *On Liberty* during the same years that he rewrote the *Autobiography*.

Whether Mill was aware of it or not, the echoes of that early experience reverberate through the pages of *On Liberty*. In this sense, *On Liberty* stands as a decisive rebuttal of his father. For it is here, more than in any other work, that he tried to provide an alternative view of man and society which would take proper account of both the 'intellectual culture' – reason and truth – and the 'internal culture' – the individual's feelings, passions, impulses, natural inclinations, personal idiosyncrasies. It is here that he tried to allow for the largest 'cultivation of the feelings' and where he was most wary of attempts to regulate and order 'outward circumstances'. If Mill also fell victim in this work, as some critics have claimed, to one of the fallacies of his father's method, if he tried to reduce an extremely complicated set of phenomena to an excessively simple formula, this too may testify to the ambivalence which that early crisis of faith imposed upon the whole of his later life.

3

There are not many major intellectual figures whose personal lives impinged so directly and decisively upon their intellectual lives. After his father, it was his wife who played a crucial part in what Mill called his 'mental progress'.[16] One might almost say that his wife took the place of his father.

In the aftermath of his crisis, Mill had discovered, in the poetry of Wordsworth and Goethe, and in the philosophy of Coleridge, Saint Simon and Comte, a fusion of thought and

16. ibid. p. 129.

feeling, an appreciation of the 'many-sidedness' of human nature and society, that went far to fill the vacuum created by utilitarianism.[17] But in one respect, as he confessed to one of his new friends, he was in a worse position than he had been before. He had lost the sense of community provided by the utilitarians, the assurance of a common purpose shared with others of like mind. Such personal ties as he now had were partial and limited, and he was left with a great sense of loneliness. He felt deprived, he said, of the kind of sympathy that could only come with 'perfect friendship'.[18]

This confession was made in 1829. A year later he met that perfect friend – his 'incomparable friend', as he spoke of her in his *Autobiography*[19] – in the person of Harriet Taylor. It was as if he had willed her into existence.

On the surface it was an unlikely friendship. Harriet Taylor was married, the wife of a prosperous merchant and the mother of two young children. (A third child was born soon afterwards.) Temperamentally and intellectually she was very different from Mill. It was perhaps these differences that attracted him. She represented everything that utilitarianism was not, everything that he still found wanting in his own character. Her few early writings reveal a romantic, intuitive mind, impassioned in opinion, impatient in sustained argument. She wrote poetry, fancied herself something of a bohemian, expressed 'advanced' views on the subjects of love, marriage, divorce, and the status of women, and, in one brief, unpublished essay, anticipated the main theme and even some of the details of *On Liberty*.

Mill was twenty-four and Mrs Taylor twenty-three when they met. In spite of the flat assertion in his *Autobiography* that 'it was years after my introduction to Mrs Taylor before my acquaintance with her became at all intimate or confidential',[20]

17. ibid. p. 114. For his relations with Comte, see editorial note to *On Liberty*, p. 73 below.

18. *The Earlier Letters of John Stuart Mill, 1812–1848*, ed. Francis E. Mineka, vols. XII and XIII of *Collected Works*; Toronto, 1963, vol. I, p. 30 (JSM to John Sterling, 15 April 1829).

19. *Autobiography*, p. 160.

20. ibid. p. 129.

it is evident from their correspondence that their acquaintance became intimate and confidential almost immediately. As early as 1831 a 'reconciliation' had to be effected between Mill and Mr Taylor.[21] And a love letter written by Mill to her the following year contained every convention of that genre including its being written in French.[22] The gossip about their affair (if it can be called that) finally reached his ailing father who taxed his son with being in love with another man's wife, to which the son is reported to have replied that 'he had no other feelings towards her, than he would have towards an equally able man'.[23] Mrs Taylor herself assured a German friend that she was Mill's '*Seelenfreundin*'.[24] And she advised Mill, when he was writing his *Autobiography*, to describe their relationship as one of 'strong affection, intimacy of friendship, and no impropriety'.[25] Although the historian has no reason to doubt these assurances, some of their friends and relatives apparently did, or at the very least questioned the propriety of a *Seelenfreundschaft* that so brazenly flouted convention.

For almost twenty years they maintained this relationship while she continued to be married to Mr Taylor. Mill dined at her London home, he weekended with her in the country (generally in the absence of her husband), and they took extended trips abroad together, sometimes accompanied by one of her children. (During the whole of this period Mill lived with his family in London, where he continued to work for the East India Company.) Although they professed to see nothing improper about all this, they were obviously under great strain. Her husband's tacit acquiescence was punctuated by occasional feeble protests, as when he objected to Mill's dedication of the *Principles of Political Economy* to her. (The

21. F. A. Hayek, *John Stuart Mill and Harriet Taylor: Their Friendship and Subsequent Marriage*, Chicago, 1951, p. 37 (B. E. Desainteville to John Taylor, early 1831[?]).

22. *Earlier Letters*, vol. I, p. 114 (Aug.(?), 1832).

23. Bain, p. 163.

24. Heinrich Gomperz, *Theodor Gomperz: Briefe und Aufzeichnungen*, Vienna, 1936, vol. I, p. 233.

25. Hayek, p. 196 (HT to JSM, 14–15 February 1854).

dedication finally appeared only in a limited number of gift copies.) There was the inevitable gossip among friends and relatives, and an exaggerated sense of that gossip on the part of its victims. Mrs Taylor felt ill-used by everyone, including Mill when he was insufficiently sensitive to what she took to be slights and offences. By the mid-forties, the situation had deteriorated to the point where Mill broke off relations with most of his old friends and was on very cool terms with his own family. Although Mr Taylor died in 1849, it was almost two years before they were married, evidently to allow for a proper period of mourning. And when they were finally married, Mill was so concerned about a minute irregularity in the marriage contract (he had first signed it ' J. S. Mill', and then, told to write out his full name, had squeezed in the 'John Stuart'), that he seriously proposed going through another ceremony lest there be any doubt, 'either to our own or to any other minds', about the legality of their marriage[26] – a sad commentary on the long years of their 'perfect friendship'.

If his marriage eased some of the difficulties of his life, it exacerbated others. His relations with his family became even more embittered when he fancied that his mother and sisters were tardy in paying their respects to his wife. (In fact, they had been so intimidated by him earlier when he discouraged their speaking of her that they were fearful of making any overtures after the marriage.) And when his brother presumed to mention the marriage without having been officially notified of it, Mill accused him of insolence. Nor did he and his wife forget the slights, or fancied slights, of old friends. Moving to Blackheath, a suburb of London, they retreated into even greater isolation. During the seven years of their marriage, they dined out seldom (if ever) and entertained at home fewer than half a dozen guests, most of them visitors from abroad. The only friends Mill saw were those who dropped in on him at his office or who attended the meetings of the Political

26. *The Later Letters of John Stuart Mill, 1849–1873*, ed. Francis E. Mineka and Dwight N. Lindley, vols. XIV–XVII of *Collected Works*, Toronto, 1972, vol. I, p. 96 (JSM to HM, 13 July 1852).

Economy Club. Their ill health increased their sense of isolation. Convinced they had only a short time to live, they resented more than ever any intrusions from without. When they travelled abroad, separately or together (separately because he could not always leave his job to accompany her, or because she was too sick to accompany him), it was usually for reasons of convalescence. But whether abroad or at home, they were almost entirely withdrawn from the literary, social, and political circles they might have been expected to frequent.

Speaking of this period of his life in the *Autobiography*, Mill explained why a person of a 'really high class of intellect' would choose to have so few relations with 'society' as to be 'almost considered as retiring from it altogether'. Society, he said, was 'insipid'; it discouraged serious discussion; it was useful only to social climbers, while those already at the top could no more than comply with the customs and demands of their station; but worst of all, it was debasing to the intellectual, whose feelings, opinions, and principles could only be lowered by contact with it. That he was describing his own situation is evident from his concluding remarks: 'All these circumstances united, made the number very small of those whose society, and still more whose intimacy, I now voluntarily sought'.[27]

If this suspicion of 'society' accounts for the peculiar nature of Mill's life during the period of his marriage, it also illuminates important aspects of *On Liberty* – which was written during this same period. The animus against society expressed in this book, the exaltation of the individual, the overweening distrust of conformity, convention, and social pressures of all kinds, correspond to the existential reality of his own life. This is not to say that the argument of the book can be explained in terms of his personal situation; only that his personal situation may have made him more receptive to that argument, may have inclined him to a more impassioned and extreme statement of it.

27. *Autobiography*, pp. 159–60.

4

On Liberty, indeed, had its origin in a project that grew out of their special sense of themselves as two beleaguered souls who were alone capable of resisting the pressures of mediocrity and of aspiring to the highest reaches of thought. It was in August 1853, during their first separation since their marriage (his wife had gone to the country to recover from a particularly bad bout of tuberculosis), that Mill alluded to a plan they had evidently discussed before: a volume of essays on subjects of crucial importance which would contain 'the best we have got to say'. 'I do not see what living depositary there is likely to be of our thoughts, or who in this weak generation that is growing up will even be capable of thoroughly mastering and assimilating your ideas, much less of reoriginating them – so we must write them and print them, and then they can wait till there are again thinkers.'[28] Some months later, after they had both suffered serious attacks, he spoke with even greater urgency of the need to get together their 'best thoughts' for the edification of posterity: 'Two years, well employed, would enable us I think to get the most of it into a fit state for print-ing – if not in the best form for popular effect, yet in the state of concentrated thought – a sort of mental pemmican, which thinkers, when there are any after us, may nourish themselves with and then dilute for other people.'[29]

This image of a 'mental pemmican' is truly extraordinary. Like the American Indian pounding together a mixture of meats, nuts and fruits to make the cakes that were his basic staple, so Mill and his wife set about to prepare the concen-trated essence of their wisdom, which intellectuals ('when there are any after us') could partake of directly, and ordinary people in diluted form. The image is all the more startling because it was unlike Mill, who was generally, indeed excessively, modest about his abilities. But he was never modest about his wife. And it was her health that worried him, the fear of her death

28. *Later Letters*, vol. I, p. 112 (30 August 1853).
29. ibid. pp. 141-42 (29 January 1854).

that made him so anxious. If she should, by ill-chance, pre-decease him, he assured her he would continue their work as best he could. But that best was not good enough. 'For even if the wreck I should be could work on with undiminished faculties, my faculties at the best are not adequate to the highest subjects.' All he could promise to do was to complete the work as she might have written it, 'for my only rule of life *then* would be what I thought you would wish as it now is what you tell me you wish.' '*I am not fit*,' he emphasized, 'to write on anything but the outskirts of the great questions of feeling and life without you to prompt me as well as to keep me right.'[30]

'Liberty' was one of eleven subjects tentatively proposed for the volume that was to be their bequest to posterity, their 'mental pemmican'. It is interesting that it was not high on their original list; nor was it the first to be actually written. But it was probably the only essay of this period that was written, at least in its original version, entirely while they were together. That early draft (which, unfortunately, has not been preserved) was completed some time in 1854. In December of that year Mill went abroad for an extended period of con-valescence (combined with a most arduous tour of sightseeing), and it was then that the subject of liberty first assumed a larger importance in his own mind.

In his *Autobiography* Mill somewhat dramatized the circum-stances in which it first occurred to him to expand the essay into a separate book. The idea, he wrote, came to him while he was 'mounting the steps of the Capitol'[31] – perhaps an uncon-scious echo of another classic which had been conceived in that historic site: *The Decline and Fall of the Roman Empire*, which Gibbon had decided upon as he sat 'musing amidst the ruins of the Capitol, while the barefooted friars were singing vespers in the Temple of Jupiter'.[32] In fact, a letter by Mill to his wife at the time suggested that he had thought of a volume

30. ibid. p. 168 (February 1854).
31. *Autobiography*, p. 170.
32. Edward Gibbon, *Autobiography*, ed. Lord Sheffield, World's Classics ed.; London, 1950, p. 160.

on liberty while he was en route to Rome (the letter itself was written before he had yet visited the Capitol), and that the idea may even have been considered by both of them earlier, probably during the writing of the original essay.

On my way here cogitating thereon [on his writing] I came back to an idea we have talked about and thought that the best thing to write and publish at present would be a volume on Liberty. So many things might be brought into it and nothing seems to me more needed – it is a growing need too, for opinion tends to encroach more on liberty, and almost all the projects of social reformers in these days are really *liberticide* – Comte, particularly so. I wish I had brought with me here the paper on Liberty that I wrote for our volume of Essays – perhaps my dearest will kindly read it through and tell me whether it will do as the foundation of one part of the volume in question – if she thinks so I will try to write and publish it in 1856 if my health permits as I hope it will.[33]

After he received the approval of his wife, he became more enthusiastic about the potentialities of the subject and invested it with a greater sense of urgency, not only because of its intrinsic importance but also because of his growing intimations of mortality.

We have got a power of which we must try to make a good use during the few years of life we have left. The more I think of the plan of a volume on Liberty, the more likely it seems to me that it will be read and make a sensation. The title itself with any known name to it would sell an edition. We must cram into it as much as possible of what we wish not to leave unsaid.[34]

Mill returned from that trip (their last prolonged separation) in June 1855. During the following year and a half he worked on *On Liberty*, as well as on his *Autobiography*. In December 1856 he reported to his publisher that he expected to finish it in time for publication the following May. After that he spoke of it occasionally to correspondents, sometimes as if it were completed, at other times as if it were nearly so, first promising it for publication in the winter of 1857–8, then postponing it without explanation. In October 1858 Mill finally retired from

33. *Later Letters*, vol. I, p. 294 (15 January 1855).
34. ibid. p. 332 (17 February 1855).

the East India Office after thirty-five years of service. He and his wife left for the south of France on the 12th. Within a week Mrs Mill was taken ill, and on 3 November 1858 she died at Avignon. Mill's first task after the funeral was to purchase a cottage overlooking the graveyard at Avignon where she was buried and to install in it the furniture from the hotel room in which she had died; it was there that he and his stepdaughter retired for several months every year for the remainder of his life. Within a week of his return to England he informed his publisher that *On Liberty* was ready for publication. It finally appeared in February 1859.

5

The genesis and history of *On Liberty* have an important bearing upon an understanding of the book itself. It is quite evident that on his own Mill would have published it long before, as he would also have published the other essays written or edited during the period of his marriage. That nothing of consequence was published during those seven and a half years, and that within months of his wife's death Mill did start to release one after another of those writings, testifies to the influence of his wife in this matter as in so many others. It was as if she were reluctant to part with the pemmican that was their life's work, just as she was loath to share their lives with friends or 'society' at large. (It is noteworthy that after her death Mill quickly renewed old friendships, took an active part in public affairs, and even accepted an invitation to stand for Parliament, an offer he had turned down shortly after his marriage.)

That they both looked upon the pemmican in general, and *On Liberty* in particular, as their 'joint production' is evident from their correspondence as well as from Mill's repeated statements to that effect in his *Autobiography* and in the dedication to *On Liberty*. One may be tempted to discount the latter, with its fulsome tributes to his wife as 'the inspirer, and in part the author, of all that is best in my writings', its assertion that this book, like all his recent works, 'belongs as much to her as to me', and its obeisance before her superior wisdom: 'Were I but capable of interpreting to the world one half the great thoughts and noble feelings which are buried in her grave, I should be the medium of a greater benefit to it, than is ever likely to arise from anything that I can write, un-prompted and unassisted by her all but unrivalled wisdom.'[35] Such sentiments, it might be thought, are the conventional pieties of dedications, especially those composed by a recently bereaved and frankly adoring husband. But Mill made the same claims too often, during her lifetime and long afterwards, to permit us to dismiss them so lightly. Moreover he spelled them out in detail, analysed the precise nature of her contributions to their joint works, and specified the particular quality of mind that was 'emphatically hers' and that was especially characteristic of *On Liberty*. The *Autobiography* deserves to be quoted at length because only thus can one appreciate the full extent of his claims on her behalf.

The *Liberty* was more directly and literally our joint production than anything else which bears my name, for there was not a sentence of it that was not several times gone through by us together, turned over in many ways, and carefully weeded of any faults, either in thought or expression, that we detected in it. It is in consequence of this that, although it never underwent her final revision, it far surpasses, as a mere specimen of composition, anything which has proceeded from me either before or since. With regard to the thoughts, it is difficult to identify any particular part or element as being more hers than all the rest. The whole mode of thinking of which the book was the expression, was emphatically hers. But I also was so thoroughly imbued with it, that the same thoughts naturally occurred to us both. That I was thus penetrated with it, however, I owe in a great degree to her . . .

The *Liberty* is likely to survive longer than anything else that I have written (with the possible exception of the *Logic*), because the conjunction of her mind with mine has rendered it a kind of philosophic text-book of a single truth, which the changes progressively taking place in modern society tend to bring out into even stronger

35. p. 58 below.

relief: the importance, to man and society, of a large variety in types of character, and of giving full freedom to human nature to expand itself in innumerable and conflicting directions . . .

After my irreparable loss, one of my earliest cares was to print and publish the treatise, so much of which was the work of her whom I had lost, and consecrate it to her memory. I have made no alteration or addition to it, nor shall I ever. Though it wants the last touch of her hand, no substitute for that touch shall ever be attempted by mine.[36]

When the *Autobiography* appeared after Mill's death, many of his friends were distressed by what they took to be the excessiveness of his praise – effusions which they thought unworthy of him, reflecting upon his good judgment and common sense. And most biographers and commentators since have ignored these passages, on the tacit assumption that Mill could not have meant them seriously, or that he had been so blinded by love that they are best passed over in embarrassed silence. But this is to confuse two distinct questions: the question of the quality of Mrs Mill's mind (in other passages of the *Autobiography* and on other occasions Mill was even more extravagant, attributing to her a genius of the highest philosophical as well as practical order); and the question of the nature and extent of her influence on his writings. The first question is the more easily answered. It is safe to say that no one could have had all the virtues, and each to an incomparable degree, which he attributed to her. Moreover what evidence we have seems to belie some of these virtues (extreme modesty and selflessness, for example), and fails to bear out others (an intellect unparalleled in her time). But the second question, the problem of her influence, is more difficult. Here, with whatever reservations and qualifications, we may be more inclined to attend to Mill's words – if only because it helps us explain the particular quality of *On Liberty* as well as important discrepancies between *On Liberty* and other of his writings.

In other passages of the *Autobiography*. Mill elucidated the

36. *Autobiography*, pp. 176–80.

particular 'mode of thinking' that was 'emphatically hers': her 'boldness of speculation', her ability to pierce to the 'very heart and marrow' of every problem, her instinct for 'always seizing the essential idea or principle'. When he said that 'the conjunction of her mind with mine has rendered it a kind of philosophic textbook of a single truth', he meant that his contribution was to make of it a philosophic text-book, hers to provide the single truth.[37]

That 'single truth' had been expressed by Harriet Mill (then Harriet Taylor) long before, in a short, unpublished essay written early in their acquaintance. She had then vigorously attacked 'society' for fostering a 'spirit of conformity' that was fatal to 'individual character'. Although there is no evidence that the essay was actually consulted by Mill at the time he wrote *On Liberty* (the manuscript was, however, available to him and was found among his effects after his death), the similarities are too striking to pass unnoticed. It is not only the main theme of her essay that is so suggestive: the varieties of conformity – religious, political, moral, and social – which are imposed by the 'opinion of Society', the collective 'mass', the 'indolently minded man', and which are implacably hostile to 'any manifestation of mental independence'. Even more revealing are some of the peripheral aspects of her paper. Anyone familiar with *On Liberty* must be struck by her argument for eccentricity: 'If by principle is intended the only useful meaning of the word, accordance of the individual's conduct with the individual's self-formed opinion . . . then eccentricity should be prima facie evidence for the existence of principle'; or by her defence of any strong conviction however erroneous it might be: 'The capability of even serious error, proves the capacity for proportionate good. For if anything may be called a principle of nature this seems to be one, that force of any kind has an intuitive tendency towards good'.[38]

37. ibid. pp. 131–2, 175.
38. Hayek, pp. 275–9.

6

The 'single truth' Mill referred to in his *Autobiography* appeared in *On Liberty* as 'one very simple principle'.

The object of this Essay is to assert one very simple principle, as entitled to govern absolutely the dealings of society with the individual in the way of compulsion and control, whether the means used be physical force in the form of legal penalties, or the moral coercion of public opinion. That principle is, that the sole end for which mankind are warranted, individually or collectively, in interfering with the liberty of action of any of their number, is self-protection. That the only purpose for which power can be rightfully exercised over any member of a civilised community, against his will, is to prevent harm to others. His own good, either physical or moral, is not a sufficient warrant. He cannot rightfully be compelled to do or forbear because it will be better for him to do so, because it will make him happier, because, in the opinions of others, to do so would be wise, or even right. These are good reasons for remonstrating with him, or reasoning with him, or persuading him, or entreating him, but not for compelling him, or visiting him with any evil in case he do otherwise. To justify that, the conduct from which it is desired to deter him must be calculated to produce evil to someone else. The only part of the conduct of anyone, for which he is amenable to society, is that which concerns others. In the part which merely concerns himself, his independence is, of right, absolute. Over himself, over his own body and mind, the individual is sovereign.[39]

If, as Mill said in the *Autobiography*, every sentence in the book was gone over by his wife and himself, not once but several times, to make certain that it said precisely what they wanted it to convey, this paragraph, which so forthrightly calls attention to itself as containing the essence of the book, is surely deserving of the closest study. It also requires careful reading because it is by now so familiar to us that its meaning can only be recaptured by a deliberate effort. Whether because this passage has been so often anthologized, or because its terms and concepts have become, by a process of cultural

39. p. 68–9 below.

osmosis, so much a part of our thinking, we tend to be inured to it, to take it for granted as an unproblematic statement of an eminently reasonable position. Yet it was in Mill's day, and remains so today in spite of its general acceptance, a bold assertion of a very radical doctrine. Some of its boldness is reflected in its language, the repeated use of such words as: one, sole, only, own, absolute, and absolutely. And the final sentence could well stand as the epigraph of modernity: 'Over himself, over his own body and mind, the Individual is sovereign.'

The rest of the book was by way of elaboration, specification, and illustration of this 'one very simple principle'. In one sphere after another – thought, discussion, and action – Mill sought to establish the necessity and sufficiency of the principle of liberty: that the liberty of the individual should be absolute except in the one case where that liberty did harm to another. On no other ground except harm could any other individual, group of individuals, or society at large presume to interfere with the individual. And interference was defined in the largest possible sense, as including not only physical and legal sanctions but also social pressures, the 'moral coercion of public opinion'. Such sanctions and pressures were illegitimate whether they were directed for or against any religious, intellectual, scientific or moral belief, or any mode of action, conduct, behaviour, or way of life – always with the one exception about harm.

This one qualification involved Mill in difficulties which have troubled commentators and critics, in his time and since. Sometimes Mill used words such as 'concern', 'affect', and 'regard' to express the qualification – as if actions which concerned, affected, or regarded another properly came within the province of society and therefore could be prohibited or discouraged by society, whereas actions which concerned, affected, or regarded only the person performing those actions were entirely within the province of the individual. This neutral set of words – concern, affect and regard – obviously of much larger extension, gave a far greater latitude to society, than the negatively charged words Mill used on other occasions – harm, hurt, injury, mischief, evil. A closer examination of the context, however, and a consideration of his examples and illustrations, suggests that when Mill said concern, affect, or regard, he meant concern, affect, or regard another *adversely*, harmfully. In this negative sense, the effect was to limit and minimize the occasions when society could legitimately interfere with the liberty of the individual.

Another common problem in the interpretation of *On Liberty* may also have been much exaggerated. It is often assumed that *On Liberty* must be judged as an exercise in the philosophy of utilitarianism, and that its success or failure depends upon its application of utilitarian criteria and the adequacy of those criteria. Thus one critic may object that Mill failed to demonstrate that liberty would necessarily contribute either to the greatest happiness of the individual or to the greatest happiness of the greatest number. Another may object that Mill did just that, and in doing so made of liberty a means rather than an end, thereby demeaning liberty itself. Another may point out the contradictions between the utilitarian and non-utilitarian parts of his argument. And still another may commend him for putting the case for liberty on the only sound, consistent, rational – that is, utilitarian – grounds, thus avoiding such dubious metaphysical principles as natural or absolute rights.

Much of this controversy is beside the point. Whatever Mill's intentions elsewhere – in his book on *Utilitarianism*, for example – it was not his intention here, in *On Liberty*, to rest his case on utilitarian principles. He occasionally, very occasionally, used the word 'utility', more often 'interests'; but he also used such non-utilitarian words as 'rights' and 'development'. In any event, his primary concern was to establish liberty, not utility, as the sole principle governing the relations of the individual and society. If any distinction between means and ends can be made, one might say that he sometimes spoke as though liberty were the means and individuality – not happiness – the end. To be sure, he assumed that 'well-being' was a by-product, perhaps even an essential ingredient, of individuality; but as he interpreted it, well-being was significantly different from happiness, still more from any calculus of pleasure and pain. Had he intended happiness to be the end, he could never have precluded society, as he did in that crucial passage in the introduction, from compelling an individual to do something, or preventing him from doing it, 'because it will make him happier'. In the utilitarian scheme it was precisely the function of the legislator to do that which would make individuals, singly and collectively, happier – which is why Bentham himself had utter contempt for the idea of liberty. Mill, by contrast, insisted that happiness was no more cause for interference with liberty than wisdom or virtue or mere conformity to the conventions of society.

It is also sometimes argued – and this raises a more serious issue that goes to the heart of *On Liberty* – that although Mill professed to make liberty, and its corollary, individuality, the supreme principle governing social relations, he was less interested in that principle itself than in the purposes it could serve, that liberty was the means for the achievement of other ends: truth, or morality, or a fully developed person, or a progressive society. Isolated sentences of *On Liberty* can certainly be read in this sense. And certainly it was Mill's hope, and it constituted a large part of his argument, that liberty and individuality would encourage and ultimately contribute to the promotion of these other ends. But Mill's essential argument – the burden of his book and the message that communicated itself to his contemporaries as well as to later generations – was the need to establish liberty and individuality so firmly and absolutely in and for themselves, to make them so completely the determinants of social policy, the test of all social action, that they would not be subject to other more proximate purposes. In each area he examined, Mill went out of his way to establish them as the necessary and sufficient ends even if it should appear that they conflicted with other ends.

Mill's case for freedom of discussion, for example, while much concerned with the question of truth, goes so far in making liberty pre-eminent that ultimately truth itself is defined in terms of liberty. Short of denying truth itself – that is, short of a relativism or nihilism that denies the very idea of truth – he could not have done more to assert the absolute supremacy of liberty in matters concerning truth. Mill himself was not a relativist or nihilist; he accepted the idea of objective truth and he believed men to be capable of attaining truths. But this makes his argument even more extraordinary. For at one point after another he made liberty the necessary and sufficient condition for all inquiry. He did this not only in the obvious case where the received opinion might be wholly or partially untrue, so that the liberty of dissenting opinion was required as a corrective to falsity; but also in those cases where the received opinion was wholly true and the dissenting opinion wholly false. Here error itself, even the dissemination of error, became a virtue. Without the competition and collision of opinion, he argued, truth degenerated into 'dead dogma'. He was so impressed by the need for competing opinions, for a vigorous adversary situation, that he was willing to encourage the artificial contrivance of opinion, of erroneous opinion, when such opinion did not naturally exist: 'So essential is this discipline to a real understanding of moral and human subjects, that if opponents of all important truths do not exist, it is indispensable to imagine them, and supply them with the strongest arguments which the most skilful devil's advocate can conjure up.'[40]

In one sense it can be said that it was for the sake, if not of truth itself, then for the vitality of truth that Mill was urging the largest possible freedom of opinion, including erroneous opinion. But while this was perhaps his intent, the immediate and direct effect of his doctrine was to make liberty rather than truth paramount. It was liberty, not truth, that society was charged with promoting; indeed society was explicitly prohibited from promoting truth itself. And it was liberty, not truth, that was the true mark of individuality; the dissenter from truth, if that truth happened to be a conventional one, was expressing his individuality as surely, perhaps more surely, than the proponent of that truth.

Mill's argument for liberty of action – the greatest possible

40. ibid. pp. 97–9.

expression of individuality – exactly paralleled his argument for liberty of discussion. In both cases, liberty rather than some other end was the final principle, the test and arbiter of individual and social behaviour. Just as he assumed that truth would emerge from liberty, so he assumed that all kinds of goods – the fullest development of the individual, virtue, vigour, even genius – would emerge from the cultivation of individuality. But it was individuality itself and the conditions making for individuality – variety, diversity, choice – that were the operative conditions of his doctrine. And just as earlier he defended liberty of discussion even when it meant liberty for error, so here he defended 'eccentricity', 'peculiarity', 'spontaneity', 'originality', 'variety', 'diversity', 'impulse', 'passion', 'experiments of living', and whatever else made for individuality, regardless of the nature or value of any particular eccentricity, peculiarity, impulse, experiment, or expression of individuality. By the same token, the antitheses to these qualities – conformity, obedience, restraint, discipline, custom, tradition, public opinion, and social pressure – were suspect in themselves, regardless of what it was that was being conformed to, obeyed, restrained, etc. The hope for the future, Mill concluded, and clearly the purpose of his own book, was to convince the 'intelligent part of the public' of the value of individuality *per se* – 'to see that it is good there should be differences, even though not for the better, even though, as it may appear to them, some should be for the worse'.[41]

7

There is much else in *On Liberty*, especially in the chapter on 'Applications', that has provided endless matter for speculation, interpretation, criticism, and commendation.

For over a century, philosophers, social critics, historians, and biographers have argued, often at inordinate length, about the meaning and validity of his doctrine. Yet the controversy has not advanced much beyond the point it reached in Mill's

41. ibid. p. 140.

own time. *On Liberty* did attain, as Mill hoped it would, the status of an instant classic. This meant that it was accepted respectfully, seriously, as one of the most important tracts of the time, some thought of all time. It did not, however, mean that it was received uncritically. On the contrary, it was subjected to the searching inquiry that was the proper due of so worthy a book.

If most of the problems discussed today in connection with *On Liberty* were anticipated by Mill's contemporaries, one point that was much controverted then is rarely alluded to today. Yet it is at the heart of Mill's doctrine. This is his description of the state of public opinion in his own time and his predictions about the probable course of its development. The reason he had been provoked to write *On Liberty*, he had said, the reason a new doctrine of liberty had become so urgent, was the new form of tyranny that was confronting mankind. The old, familiar tyranny of despotic government, in which rulers imposed their will upon the ruled, had ceased to be a threat in civilized society boasting representative or popular government, where the interest and will of rulers was becoming more and more identified with the interest and will of the ruled. But it was precisely the rise of popular government that he saw as the pre-condition of a new and more formidable despotism. For the 'tyranny of the majority' was now exerting itself not so much in politics as in the entire area of social life. 'Society is itself the tyrant', and more oppressive than any tyrant of old because 'it leaves fewer means of escape, penetrating much more deeply into the details of life, and enslaving the soul itself'.[42] It imposes a new 'despotism of custom';[43] it dictates its will by means of public opinion; it presumes to tell men what to think and read, how to dress and behave; it sets itself up as the judge of right and wrong, propriety and impropriety; it discourages spontaneity and originality, personal impulses and desires, strong character and unconventional ideas; it is fatal, in short, to individuality. And all of this, Mill predicted, was bound to get worse as the public more and more felt its power and acted upon it. Only

42. ibid. p. 63.   43. ibid. p. 136.

the most rigorous doctrine of liberty and the largest assertion of the sovereignty of the individual could prevent England from becoming 'another China', the terrible 'warning example' of a civilization which from the best of motives, the desire to impose a single model of virtue and wisdom upon everyone, had succeeded in bringing all progress to a halt.[44]

It was this view of a 'social tyranny' leading to a fatal decline of individuality that most reviewers challenged. Some questioned the fact of a decline of individuality. Others granted the fact but denied that the tyranny of society was responsible for the decline. Even H. T. Buckle, author of the recently published *History of Civilization in England* (1857), qualified his lavish praise of Mill by entering one small demur. He could not agree that individuality had diminished nor that it was likely to do so in the future. In this respect as in most others, he was confident England was advancing inexorably along the road of reason and progress. But he recognized that other serious thinkers shared Mill's fears, and that in any event it was salutary to be reminded of a potential evil which might otherwise be ignored.[45]

James Fitzjames Stephen, who is famous for his later book-length attack on Mill, was at first attracted to the thesis of *On Liberty*. Reviewing the book in two successive editions of the *Saturday Review*, he devoted the first part to what amounted to a eulogy of Mill for recalling Englishmen to the principle of liberty which they had thought 'established beyond the reach of controversy'. This principle, he agreed with Mill, was being undermined by a powerful, irresistible tyranny which was contributing to 'the gradual destruction of all the peculiarities of individuals, and the general adoption of a sort of commonplace ideal of character, to which everyone is forced to conform, by a vast variety of petty sanctions applying with a leaden invariable persistency to all the common actions of life'.[46] The second part of the review, however, as if to gainsay

44. ibid. p. 137.
45. *Frazer's Magazine*, vol. LIX (1859), pp. 526–33.
46. *Saturday Review*, vol. VII (1859), p. 186.

the first, suggested that this 'melancholy' view of affairs (several reviewers used the word melancholy in describing the tone or message of *On Liberty*) was only part of the truth. Individuality was, to be sure, as important as Mill said it was, and intolerance was as abhorrent. But the conformity that society exacted was for the most part of a limited and not very onerous kind. In the most important areas of life, freedom was more available and individuality more widespread than ever before. A person might be obliged to wear a coat of a particular cut, to shave, and to observe certain conventions about what could or could not be said in mixed company. But this was a small 'quit-rent' for the privilege of reading what he pleased, thinking what he liked, educating his children in a manner of his choosing, and adopting any or no religious creed. In important matters such as these, 'there probably never was a time when men who have any sort of originality or independence of character had it in their power to hold the world at arm's length so cheaply'.[47] A fortnight later the *Review* revoked even this small concession about the lack of individuality in the trivial matters of life. It then pointed out that beards were being flaunted, 'unprotected females' were stalking across Europe, tobacco was breaking through the 'decorum of heavy respectability', and in dozens of other ways eccentricity was becoming so commonplace it was 'ceasing to be eccentric'.[48]

Other reviewers found different cause for disagreement. The *National Review*, for example (in an essay possibly written by Walter Bagehot), conceded that public opinion had become more 'homogeneous', reflecting fewer conflicting modes of thought and fewer divergent social types. But so far from interpreting this 'moral monotony' as a threat to liberty, it saw it rather as the necessary and commendable result of the growth of social and political liberty. What were disappearing were not individual varieties of character but sharply demarcated social types, the highly distinctive types associated with class, region, and sect. But it was precisely because individual freedom had increased that these social types had lost their

47. ibid. p. 213.   48. ibid. pp. 269–70.

intensity. Nothing had been more 'exigeant and irritating in its despotism' than the sectarianism and provincialism of local groups. The decline of the various forms of local despotism, each with its own stringent code of opinion and custom, had indeed led to a greater similarity of thought and behaviour, but this derived from a far larger social base than the old codes and was less oppressive in its effect upon the individual. The *National Review* also warned against Mill's remedy for the loss of individuality; the complete withdrawal of society and public opinion from the affairs of individuals would only aggravate the evil, since an excessive laxity of the social bond was as detrimental to true individuality as an excessive rigour of that bond.[49]

One reviewer objected that a doctrine like Calvinism, which Mill took to be repressive of individuality, actually stimulated individuality by fostering the development of a strong and energetic character.[50] Another quoted against Mill his own essay on Coleridge, which had emphasized the importance of national as well as individual character, and which had made the social bond a necessary ingredient of individual well-being. The same critic insisted that there was no want of freedom of thought for those capable of using it, that any serious thinker could get a hearing for any idea on any subject however unconventional: 'A generation which has produced and which has listened attentively to Mr Carlyle, Mr Froude and Mr Buckle cannot be charged with shrinking blindly from independence of thought.'[51] Another reviewer cited the popularity of Mill himself as evidence of both the exercise of independent thought and respect for it. Indeed he found the tone of Mill's book curiously out of keeping with its source: 'It might almost indeed have come from the prison-cell of some persecuted thinker bent on making one last protest against the growing tyranny of the public mind, though conscious that his appeal will be in vain – instead of from the pen of a writer who has perhaps exercised more influence over the formation of the

49. *National Review*, vol. VIII (1859), pp. 393–424.
50. *Saturday Review*, vol. VII (1859), p. 214.
51. *Bentley's Quarterly Review*, vol. XI (1860), p. 442.

philosophical and social principles of cultivated Englishmen than any other man of his generation.'[52]

It was in the same spirit that Macaulay wrote about *On Liberty* in his journal:

What is meant by the complaint that there is no individuality now? Genius takes its own course, as it always did. Bolder invention was never known in science than in our time. The steam-ship, the steam-carriage, the electric telegraph, the gaslights, the new military engines, are instances. Geology is quite a new true science. Phrenology is quite a new false one. Whatever may be thought of the theology, the metaphysics, the political theories of our time, boldness and novelty are not what they want. Comtism, Saint-Simonianism, Fourierism, are absurd enough, but surely they are not indications of a servile respect for usage and authority. Then the clairvoyance, the spirit-rapping, the table-turning, and all those other dotages and knaveries, indicate rather a restless impatience of the beaten paths than a stupid determination to plod on in those paths. Our lighter literature, as far as I know it, is spasmodic and eccentric. Every writer seems to aim at doing something odd – at defying all rules and canons of criticism. The metre must be queer; the diction queer. So great is the taste of oddity that men who have no recommendation but oddity hold a high place in vulgar estimation. I therefore do not at all like to see a man of Mill's excellent abilities recommending eccentricity as a thing almost good in itself – as tending to prevent us from sinking into that Chinese, that Byzantine, state which I should agree with him in considering a great calamity. He is really crying 'Fire!' in Noah's flood.[53]

8

As subsequent editions of *On Liberty* were published – six in Mill's lifetime, all unchanged, as he had promised in tribute to his wife, by so much as a word – so the commentaries continued to appear, culminating in the full-length critique by James Fitzjames Stephen in 1872, several months before Mill's

52. *National Review*, vol. VIII (1859), p. 393.
53. G. O. Trevelyan, *The Life and Letters of Lord Macaulay*, New York, 1876, vol. II, pp. 385–6.

death. Only one part, but the larger part, of *Liberty, Equality, Fraternity* was specifically concerned with *On Liberty*; the rest dealt more with Mill's *Utilitarianism* and his essay on the *Subjection of Women*.

It was on utilitarian grounds, or what he took to be such, that Stephen based his criticisms. Since the motives governing human behaviour were pain and pleasure, fear and hope, society had to utilize all its resources to direct those motives towards socially desirable ends. It had not only a right but a duty to invoke whatever social and religious sanctions were available to it: legal punishment and the fear of damnation, social approbation and the hope for salvation. Mill's doctrine, a form of moral laissez-fairism in which each individual was encouraged to do as he liked so long as he did not injure another, failed to distinguish between good and bad, let alone to give effect to that distinction. It was also a denial of the whole of history, in which the progress of civilization depended upon the expedient use of moral, religious, and legal coercion. As wisdom and virtue required the active support of society, so, Stephen reasoned, did truth. Had Mill been content to argue that in that time and place the discussion of most controversial questions should be completely free and without legal restraint, Stephen would have had no objection. But in trying to establish freedom of discussion as the prerequisite of truth, Mill was doing more than asserting the desirability of a particular social policy; he was making a metaphysical statement about the nature of truth, assuming truth to be necessarily inconsistent with authority and necessarily the product of free discussion, an assumption which Stephen found to be highly dubious. Equally dubious was the supposition that free discussion was a means of vitalizing truth; as often as not, such discussion had a debilitating and ennervating effect. Nor was Mill warranted in making the liberty of action essential to the development of individuality, nor in attributing any merit to individuality itself. 'Though goodness is various,' Stephen observed, 'variety is not in itself good.' He quoted an example his brother, Leslie Stephen, had used in a recent article on Mill: 'A nation in which everybody was sober would be a happier, better, and more progressive, though a less diversified, nation than one in which half the members were sober and the other half habitual drunkards.'[54] Mill, Stephen concluded, had elevated liberty and individuality to the status of absolute ends instead of judging them pragmatically, expedientially, in terms of their utility under particular conditions. Liberty was no more good in and of itself than was fire; like fire it was 'both good and bad according to time, place, and circumstance'.[55]

From the perspective of *On Liberty*, Stephen's book seems to be propounding something like a counter-doctrine to liberty – an invitation, perhaps, to the very 'social tyranny' Mill had feared. In fact, it was only in theory and on principle that Stephen allowed to society a large latitude regarding moral, religious, and social sanctions. In practice, he was not counselling that society avail itself of this latitude; on the contrary, he believed that England at that time had no great need for such sanctions. What disturbed him about Mill's doctrine was the possibility that its adoption would leave society impotent in those situations where there was a genuine need for social action. Implicit too was the possibility that the withdrawal of social sanctions against any particular belief or act would be interpreted as a sanctioning of that belief or act, a licence to do that which society could not prohibit.

Stephen's book provoked another round of controversy, his Hobbesian view of human nature and society alienating many who might have been responsive to a different kind of critique. Mill himself, who had always found Stephen arrogant and 'brutal',[56] thought the book would prove more damaging to Stephen than to himself. He 'does not know what he is arguing against,' Mill said, 'and is more likely to repel than to attract people.'[57] Whatever the justice of Mill's comment, or of

54. James Fitzjames Stephen, *Liberty, Equality, Fraternity*, ed. R. J. White, Cambridge, 1967, p. 80. The quote is from Leslie Stephen, 'Social Macadamisation', *Fraser's Magazine*, vol. LXXXVI (1872), p. 150.

55. J. F. Stephen, p. 85.

56. *Later Letters*, vol. IV, p. 1600 (JSM to E. E. Cliffe Leslie, 8 May 1869).

57. Bain, p. 111.

Stephen's criticisms of Mill, it was *On Liberty* that continued to be read and reprinted while *Liberty, Equality, Fraternity* soon lapsed into obscurity, enjoying a *sub rosa* reputation among a few scholars and thinkers.

A century after the publication of *On Liberty*, the controversy between Mill and Stephen surfaced again when H. L. A. Hart, then Professor of Jurisprudence at Oxford, remarked upon the striking similarity between Stephen's arguments and those recently advanced by Lord Devlin in an essay on *The Enforcement of Morals*. The occasion for Devlin's essay was the Report of the Wolfenden Commission recommending the legalization of homosexuality between consenting adults. Against the Commission's claim that private morality and immorality were 'not the law's business', Devlin argued that 'the suppression of vice is as much the law's business as the suppression of subversive activities; it is no more possible to define a sphere of private morality than it is to define one of private subversive activity'.[58] Hart, in turn, defending the Wolfenden Commission against Devlin, pointed out that its principles were essentially those of Mill and Devlin's those of Stephen.[59] (When these parallels were brought to his attention, Devlin tried to find a copy of the book that had so curiously anticipated his own position. It was only after some time and with great difficulty that he located a tattered copy in the Holborn Public Library; the book was in such bad condition that it was held together with an elastic band.)[60]

9

It is unfortunate that other more eminent Victorians did not write extended critiques of *On Liberty*, for Stephen's brand of utilitarianism was not the only basis from which *On Liberty* could be criticized. Carlyle, for example, would have judged it from a very different perspective. In a letter to his brother,

58. Patrick Devlin, *The Enforcement of Morals*, Oxford, 1968, pp. 13–14.
59. H. L. A. Hart, *Law, Liberty, and Morality*, New York, 1963, p. 16.
60. The book has since been re-issued. See footnote 54 above.

he gave his typically candid and caustic opinion of the book: 'In my life I never read a serious, ingenious, clear, logical Essay with more perfect and profound dissent from the basis it rests upon, and most of the conclusions it arrives at. Very strange to me indeed; a curious monition to me what a world we are in! As if it were a sin to control, or coerce into better methods, human swine in any way . . . *Ach Gott in Himmel*!'[61]

If John Henry Newman has left no such memorable comment on *On Liberty*, it was not because he was indifferent to it, but because it was a minor skirmish in a much larger war he was waging. His quarrel with liberalism in the *Apologia Pro Vita Sua*, published in 1864, directed itself against an attitude of mind that long antedated Mill, that went back at least to the earliest Christian heresies. His attack in the appendix to the second edition of the *Apologia* was directed primarily against religious liberalism, but it applied *a fortiori* to secular liberalism. Most of the propositions of the liberal heresy, as Newman enumerated them, could have been taken almost verbatim from *On Liberty*:

No one can believe what he does not understand.

No theological doctrine is anything more than an opinion which happens to be held by bodies of men.

It is dishonest in a man to make an act of faith in what he has not had brought home to him by actual proof.

It is immoral in a man to believe more than he can spontaneously receive as being congenial to his moral and mental nature.

There is a right of Private Judgment: that is, there is no existing authority on earth competent to interfere with the liberty of individuals in reasoning and judging for themselves about the Bible and its contents, as they severally please.

There are rights of conscience such, that everyone may lawfully advance a claim to profess and teach what is false and wrong in matters, religious, social, and moral, provided that to his private conscience it seems absolutely true and right.

There is no such thing as a national or state conscience.

61. *New Letters of Thomas Carlyle*, ed. Alexander Carlyle, London, 1904, vol. II, p. 196 (4 May 1859).

The civil power has no positive duty, in a normal state of things, to maintain religious truth.[62]

Matthew Arnold was another eminent Victorian whose work contained an implicit rather than overt critique of *On Liberty*. Oddly enough, his first reading of the book had left him rather favourably disposed to it. 'It is worth reading attentively,' he told his sister, 'being one of the few books that inculcate tolerance in an unalarming and inoffensive way.'[63] On another occasion he distinguished Mill from the crasser utilitarians who were 'doomed to sterility'; unlike them, Mill had some perception of truths that transcended utility. It was this that made him a 'writer of distinguished mark and influence', although not quite a 'great writer'.[64]

In *Culture and Anarchy*, published a decade after *On Liberty*, Arnold took a less benign view of Mill. Although he mentioned Mill only once and *On Liberty* not at all, his book was a powerful indictment of the doctrine Mill had advanced. The title of the second chapter of *Culture and Anarchy*, 'Doing as One Likes', clearly echoed one of the principles of *On Liberty*: 'liberty of tastes and pursuits, of framing the plan of our life to suit our own character, of doing as we like, subject to such consequences as may follow.'[65] To Arnold the principle that every Englishman has the 'right to do what he likes' meant in practice the 'right to march where he likes, enter where he likes, hoot as he likes, threaten as he likes, smash as he likes'.[66] Nor was Arnold better disposed to the idea that everyone has the right to say what he likes, for this involved

62. Newman, *Apologia Pro Vita Sua*, ed. A. D. Culler, Riverside ed.; Boston, 1956, pp. 275–7 (propositions 1–5, 9–12, 18).

63. *Letters of Matthew Arnold*, ed. G. W. E. Russell, New York, 1900, vol. I, p. 111 (25 June 1859).

64. Matthew Arnold, *Lectures and Essays in Criticism*, ed. R. H. Super (Ann Arbor, 1962), p. 136. For a similarly qualified view of Mill, see also Arnold's preface to the 2nd edition of 'Higher Schools and Universities in France', in *A French Eton*, London, 1892, p. 156.

65. p. 71 below.

66. *Culture and Anarchy*, ed. J. Dover Wilson, Cambridge, 1957, p. 76. *Culture and Anarchy* was first published as a volume in 1869; it had appeared serially in *Cornhill Magazine* in 1867–8.

the same provocation to anarchy and the same subversion of culture: 'The aspirations of culture are not satisfied, unless what men say, when they may say what they like, is worth saying, – has good in it, and more good than bad.'[67]

Individuality as a good in itself was as antipathetical to Arnold as liberty conceived as a good in itself. This notion of individuality violated his sense of tradition and authority, his respect for establishments (religious and political), his conception of the positive role of the state and of the integral relationship of the individual to both society and the state. But above all it was his idea of culture that militated against Mill's idea of liberty. Mill would have agreed with Arnold that culture involved 'criticism', the 'free play of mind', a disinterested 'curiosity'. But where Mill would have made of these neutral concepts capable of leading men in any direction, towards any end, Arnold infused them from the outset with substance and purpose. For Arnold the play of mind was free, curiosity was disinterested, criticism was serious, when and only when they were at the service of 'right reason', 'excellence', 'sweetness and light', 'total perfection'. In effect, virtue and wisdom, rather than liberty and individuality, were the proper ends of man. If anarchy was so fearful, it was not because it subverted this or that institution but because it subverted the culture that alone distinguished man from the animal and material world.

One must, then, look not only to reviews and critiques for the contemporary response to *On Liberty*, but also to alternative systems of thought: the *Weltanschauung* of a Carlyle, the theology of a Newman, the philosophy of an Arnold. When all these are taken into account – the unwritten, so to speak, as well as the written reviews – one can only conclude that the reaction to *On Liberty* was anything but uniformly favourable, that there were large reservations both about the argument and the basic principle of *On Liberty*.

67. ibid. p. 50.

Yet in spite of this critical response, *On Liberty* had an enormous influence upon contemporary thought. John Morley, who had been a student at Oxford at the time, later asserted: 'I do not know whether then or at any other time so short a book ever instantly produced so wide and so important an effect on contemporary thought as did Mill's *On Liberty* in that day of intellectual and social fermentation.'[68] Thomas Hardy recalled that students in the mid-sixties knew *On Liberty* 'almost by heart'.[69] And Frederic Harrison, who was himself a Comtean and therefore not much of a liberal, attributed to it a considerable practical as well as intellectual influence:

It is certain that the little book produced a profound impression on contemporary thought, and had an extraordinary success with the public. It has been read by hundreds of thousands, and, to some of the most vigorous and most conscientious spirits amongst us, it became a sort of gospel . . . It was the code of many thoughtful writers and several influential politicians. It undoubtedly contributed to the practical programmes of Liberals and Radicals for the generation that saw its birth; and the statute book bears many traces of its influence over the sphere and duties of government.[70]

Harrison may well have overstated its practical influence. Indeed he himself qualified his remarks at one point by suggesting that after 1870 Mill's influence 'waned',[71] which considerably narrows the 'generation' that presumably accepted *On Liberty* as 'gospel'. And his statement that it had contributed to the 'practical programmes of Liberals and Radicals' is difficult to accept in view of the fact that most of those programmes were designed to expand rather than restrict the area of government and social control. Yet Harrison's impres-

68. Morley, *Recollections*, vol. I, p. 60.
69. Hardy, letter to the editor of *The Times*, 21 May 1906 (p. 6).
70. Harrison, *Tennyson, Ruskin, Mill and Other Literary Estimates*, London, 1899, pp. 292–3.
71. ibid. p. 275.

sions, contradictory as they were, were typical. It is curious to find, again and again in the testimony of contemporaries, assertions about the large influence exercised by *On Liberty*, combined with expressions of personal doubts and reservations.

Charles Kingsley, for example, is often quoted as having said, and not retrospectively but at the time, that he chanced upon *On Liberty* in a bookstore, was so caught up in it that he read it then and there, and that it made him 'a clearer-headed and braver-minded man on the spot'.[72] But it never made him so clear-headed and brave-minded as to convert him to the kind of liberalism Mill was advocating. Although Kingsley was at this time less militant a socialist than he had been, he never completely abandoned his faith in socialism or embraced the individualism of *On Liberty*. (Moreover his decline of socialist zeal had set in long before his reading of *On Liberty*.) His later comment on Mill is in curious contrast to his earlier remark about clear-headedness and brave-mindedness. 'When I look at his cold, clear-cut face,' he said, after visiting Mill in 1869, 'I think there is a whole hell beneath him, of which he knows nothing, and so there may be a whole heaven above him.'[73]

John Morley, who was one of Mill's most devoted disciples, tried to account for the ambivalent response to *On Liberty* – the sense that it was enormously important and influential, and at the same time the admission that it had logical and practical flaws – by suggesting that its moral appeal was so powerful as to make its flaws seem inconsequential.[74] One might add that its moral appeal was all the more powerful precisely because of its flaws: its over-simplicity, its reductivism, its attempt to subsume a large and complicated set of problems under 'one very simple principle'. There is a boldness about simplicity, even over-simplicity, that is morally attractive, as if to defy reality, to deny complexity, is an

72. *Later Letters*, vol. II, p. 632 (JSM to Bain, 6 August 1859).

73. *Charles Kingsley: His Letters and Memories of his Life*, ed. Mrs. Kingsley, one vol. ed.; London, 1888, p. 295.

74. Morley, *Recollections*, vol. I, pp. 61–2.

assertion of moral superiority, of the power of mind over matter, of will over all the mundane and ignoble circumstances governing our lives.

II

In the century since Mill's death, the social reality has become infinitely more complicated, and to that extent Mill's principle of liberty would seem to be less applicable than ever before. Yet even as liberals have acquiesced in an unprecedented extension of social and government control, they feel more than ever committed to the principle of liberty *per se*. This principle has led to an almost schizophrenic situation, in which liberals find themselves supporting legislation and government intervention to promote economic security, or material welfare, or racial equality, or whatever else they deem to be of pressing social concern, while at the same time denying to society and government any authority over individuals in matters affecting their moral and spiritual welfare – pornography and obscenity, sexual practices and social customs, manners and morals. Pressed to justify this apparent discrepancy, liberals invoke something akin to Mill's distinction between self-regarding and other-regarding actions. In the first instance, they argue, social intervention is required because the individual is not in control of his situation and therefore may be injured by the actions of another: a car manufacturer who has not provided seat belts, an employer who offers less than a prescribed wage, a school district zoned in such a way as to segregate the races. In the second instance, it is said, social intervention is not warranted because the individual is and should be entirely in control of himself, free to indulge in whatever activities he desires, to engage in any 'experiment of living'.

That present-day liberalism has gone much further than Mill in enlarging the sphere of the other-regarding is obvious enough. Mill, after all, was a laissez-fairist, and while he admitted exceptions to that doctrine (most notably to provide for compulsory education and to prohibit the marriage of those without the means of supporting a family), he admitted them as exceptions rather than the rule.[75] It is less obvious, but none the less true, that we have also gone beyond Mill in respect to the self-regarding sphere. Mill did try to maintain, although not always successfully, a distinction we are more and more losing sight of, the distinction between the private and the public; by his account, a private act of immorality would fall within the private domain whereas the same act committed in public would constitute an 'offence against decency'.[76] He also maintained the distinction – again one we are in danger of losing – between morality and immorality. If he insisted upon the legality of private immoral acts, he did not deny the fact of their immorality. He did not argue, as many liberals do today, that there is no objective distinction between, for example, pornography and non-pornography, that such judgements are entirely subjective, entirely in the eyes of the beholder or a fiat of social convention. Mill himself was no moral relativist. His only purpose was to ensure that society be neutral in respect to private acts of immorality.

Yet in making so strong a case for social neutrality, Mill contributed to an atmosphere of moral relativism in which people call in question not only the legitimacy of social interference but also the legitimacy of moral judgement. And this, in turn, has led, and increasingly in recent years, to a denial of the distinction between private and public. If it is not possible to call private acts immoral, by what right, it is asked, can these acts be regarded as 'offences against decency' when they are committed in public?

There is a logic of ideas which does not necessarily conform to the logic of the philosopher. Society carries out ideas in ways their originator may not have foreseen nor intended. This is the meaning of Acton's admonition that men are more often the godparents of ideas than their legitimate parents. But even as godparents they have a large responsibility for their progeny. And it is in this sense that we are today living out the logic of much of *On Liberty* – with all the contradic-

75. p. 179 below.   76. ibid. p. 168.

tions, inconsistencies, and difficulties Mill's contemporaries found when they read the book over a century ago. If today most of us seem to be less aware of those difficulties, it is because the essential doctrine of *On Liberty*, the primacy of the idea of liberty, has become so much a part of our intellectual heritage that we are no longer aware of its assumptions, we no longer regard it as problematic.

Lord Asquith once described Mill – the Mill of the *Logic* and *Political Economy* – as the 'Purveyor-general of Thought for the early Victorians'.[77] *On Liberty* is not now, as the *Logic* and *Political Economy* were then, required reading for all university students or the subject of earnest disputation among thoughtful men. But it has become, perhaps by a process of cultural assimilation, the gospel of our own time even more than of Mill's day. Like all gospels, it is frequently violated in practice and even sometimes defied in principle. But liberty remains, for good and bad, the only moral principle that commands general assent in the western world. In this sense Mill has become the 'Purveyor-general of Thought' for generations which have long since discarded much of their Victorian heritage.

77. H. H. Asquith, *Some Aspects of the Victorian Age*, Oxford, 1918, p. 16.

Notes on Further Reading

A USEFUL but unfortunately not entirely complete bibliography of John Stuart Mill has been compiled, on the basis of Mill's own record, by N. MacMinn, R. Hainds, and J. M. McCrimmon (Evanston, 1944).

The *Collected Works of John Stuart Mill* are currently being published by the University of Toronto Press under the general editorship of F. E. L. Priestley and J. M. Robson. *On Liberty* has not yet been published in this series. Of the works that have appeared, those most pertinent to *On Liberty* are Mill's *Earlier Letters, 1812–1848*, ed. Francis E. Mineka, 2 vols., Toronto, 1963, and the *Later Letters, 1849–1873*, ed. Francis E. Mineka and Dwight N. Lindley, 4 vols., Toronto, 1972. These volumes reprint some of the letters first published by Friedrich A. Hayek, *John Stuart Mill and Harriet Taylor: Their Friendship and Subsequent Marriage* (Chicago, 1951). The Hayek volume, however, is still valuable, both for letters not included in the *Collected Works* (by Mrs Mill and others) and for the admirable research and commentary by Hayek.

Mill's *Autobiography* has not yet been published in the *Collected Works*. Two editions are especially useful: the Columbia University edition prepared by John Jacob Coss (New York, 1924); and *The Early Draft of John Stuart Mill's Autobiography*, ed. Jack Stillinger, Urbana, Illinois, 1961.

Among Mill's other works bearing on the themes of *On Liberty*, the most important are: *A System of Logic*, 1st edition, 1843; last and 8th edition, 1872: *Principles of Political Economy*, 1st edition, 1848; last and 7th edition, 1871; reprinted in *Collected Works*, 2 vols., Toronto, 1965; books IV and V reprinted in Pelican Classics series, London, 1970: *Considerations on Representative Government*, 1st edition 1861: *Utilitarianism*, first published serially in *Fraser's Magazine*, October–November 1861; published as a volume, 1963. Several volumes of essays are relevant: *Dissertations and Discussions*, 4 vols.,

1859–75: *Essays on Politics and Culture*, ed. Gertrude Himmel-farb, New York, 1962: *Essays on Ethics, Religion and Society*, ed. J. M. Robson, vol. X of *Collected Works*, Toronto, 1969.

The secondary works on Mill are so voluminous it is doubtful whether any bibliography could comprehend them all. The most notable biographies are those by Mill's friend, Alexander Bain, *John Stuart Mill*, New York, 1882, and the more recent, far more comprehensive work by Michael St. John Packe, *The Life of John Stuart Mill*, London, 1954. Some intellectual studies include: Leslie Stephen, *The English Utilitarians*, vol. III, London, 1900; R. P. Anschutz, *The Philosophy of J. S. Mill*, Oxford, 1951; Karl Britton, *John Stuart Mill*, Penguin edition, London, 1953; Alan Ryan, *John Stuart Mill*, London 1969. A selective list of some of the more recent literature is appended to *Mill: A Collection of Critical Essays*, ed. J. B. Schneewind, Notre Dame, 1969. One essay may be singled out for special mention: Isaiah Berlin, 'Two Concepts of Liberty', first published in 1958 and reprinted in *Four Essays on Liberty*, Oxford, 1969. A textual analysis of *On Liberty*, elaborating upon some of the points raised in the Introduction to the present Pelican edition, is Gertrude Himmelfarb's *On Liberty and Liberanism: The Case of John Stuart Mill*, New York, 1974.

Note on the Text and Title

ALL the editions of *On Liberty* published in Mill's lifetime were identical with the first, except for the correction of a few typographical errors. This was a deliberate decision on Mill's part. Since he looked upon *On Liberty* as the 'joint production' of his wife and himself, he published it, after her death, exactly as it then stood. He explained in his *Autobiography*:

After my irreparable loss, one of my earliest cares was to print and publish the treatise, so much of which was the work of her whom I had lost, and consecrate it to her memory. I have made no alteration or addition to it, nor shall I ever. Though it wants the last touch of her hand, no substitute for that touch shall ever be attempted by mine.[1]

The title is sometimes erroneously given as *Essay on Liberty*. Although Mill originally planned it as an essay to be included in a volume of essays, he later decided to expand it and publish it as a separate volume (see Introduction, page 22). When the book appeared in 1859, it bore the title *On Liberty*. Mill himself once had occasion to comment on the incorrect title. In a *Handbook of Contemporary Biography* published in 1861, his book, referred to as 'Essay on Liberty', was described as a 'rather timid defence of his early faith'. Upon receiving the proof of this volume, Mill wrote to the publisher:

If the little book 'On Liberty' is termed an Essay, the word Essay should not be in inverted commas. Whether the book is timid or not, is a matter of opinion. It has been more commonly charged with being overbold.[2]

Footnotes. In this edition, the footnotes have been arranged as follows: Mill's notes are marked by an asterisk; editorial notes are numbered 1–33. In cases where Mill's note is supplemented by an editorial comment, this appears in square brackets, directly after the author's note.

1. *Autobiography*, Columbia University ed., New York, 1924, p. 180.
2. 22 January 1860, British Museum Mss. 28511. f. 173.

ON

LIBERTY

BY

JOHN STUART MILL.

LONDON:
JOHN W. PARKER AND SON, WEST STRAND.
M.DCCC.LIX.

The grand, leading principle, towards which every argument unfolded in these pages directly converges, is the absolute and essential importance of human development in its richest diversity.

WILHELM VON HUMBOLDT,
Sphere and Duties of Government.

To the beloved and deplored memory of her who was the inspirer, and in part the author, of all that is best in my writings — the friend and wife whose exalted sense of truth and right was my strongest incitement, and whose approbation was my chief reward — I dedicate this volume. Like all that I have written for many years, it belongs as much to her as to me; but the work as it stands has had, in a very insufficient degree, the inestimable advantage of her revision; some of the most important portions having been reserved for a more careful re-examination, which they are now never destined to receive. Were I but capable of interpreting to the world one half the great thoughts and noble feelings which are buried in her grave, I should be the medium of a greater benefit to it, than is ever likely to arise from anything that I can write, unprompted and unassisted by her all but unrivalled wisdom.

CHAPTER I

Introductory

THE subject of this essay is not the so-called 'liberty of the will', so unfortunately opposed to the misnamed doctrine of philosophical necessity; but civil, or social liberty: the nature and limits of the power which can be legitimately exercised by society over the individual. A question seldom stated, and hardly ever discussed in general terms, but which profoundly influences the practical controversies of the age by its latent presence, and is likely soon to make itself recognized as the vital question of the future. It is so far from being new that, in a certain sense, it has divided mankind almost from the remotest ages; but in the stage of progress into which the more civilized portions of the species have now entered, it presents itself under new conditions and requires a different and more fundamental treatment.

The struggle between liberty and authority is the most conspicuous feature in the portions of history with which we are earliest familiar, particularly in that of Greece, Rome, and England. But in old times this contest was between subjects, or some classes of subjects, and the government. By liberty was meant protection against the tyranny of the political rulers. The rulers were conceived (except in some of the popular governments of Greece) as in a necessarily antagonistic position to the people whom they ruled. They consisted of a governing One, or a governing tribe or caste, who derived their authority from inheritance or conquest, who, at all events, did not hold it at the pleasure of the governed, and whose supremacy men did not venture, perhaps did not desire, to contest, whatever precautions might be taken against its oppressive exercise. Their power was regarded as necessary, but also as highly dangerous; as a weapon which they would attempt to use against their subjects, no less than against external enemies. To prevent the weaker members of the community from being preyed upon by innumerable vultures, it was needful that there should be an animal of prey stronger than the rest, commissioned to keep them down. But as the king of the vultures would be no less bent upon preying on the flock than any of the minor harpies, it was indispensable to be in a perpetual attitude of defence against his beak and claws. The aim, therefore, of patriots was to set limits to the power which the ruler should be suffered to exercise over the community; and this limitation was what they meant by liberty. It was attempted in two ways. First, by obtaining a recognition of certain immunities, called political liberties or rights, which it was to be regarded as a breach of duty in the ruler to infringe, and which if he did infringe, specific resistance or general rebellion was held to be justifiable. A second, and generally a later, expedient was the establishment of constitutional checks by which the consent of the community, or of a body of some sort, supposed to represent its interests, was made a necessary condition to some of the more important acts of the governing power. To the first of these modes of limitation, the ruling power, in most European countries, was compelled, more or less, to submit. It was not so with the second; and, to attain this, or, when already in some degree possessed, to attain it more completely, became everywhere the principal object of the lovers of liberty. And so long as mankind were content to combat one enemy by another, and to be ruled by a master on condition of being guaranteed more or less efficaciously against his tyranny, they did not carry their aspirations beyond this point.

A time, however, came, in the progress of human affairs, when men ceased to think it a necessity of nature that their governors should be an independent power opposed in interest to themselves. It appeared to them much better that the various magistrates of the state should be their tenants or delegates, revocable at their pleasure. In that way alone, it seemed, could they have complete security that the powers of government would never be abused to their disadvantage. By degrees this new demand for elective and temporary rulers became the prominent object of the exertions of the popular party wherever any such party existed, and superseded, to a considerable extent, the previous efforts to limit the power of rulers. As the struggle proceeded for making the ruling power emanate from the periodical choice of the ruled, some persons began to think that too much importance had been attached to the limitation of the power itself. *That* (it might seem) was a resource against rulers whose interests were habitually opposed to those of the people. What was now wanted was that the rulers should be identified with the people, that their interest and will should be the interest and will of the nation. The nation did not need to be protected against its own will. There was no fear of its tyrannizing over itself. Let the rulers be effectually responsible to it, promptly removable by it, and it could afford to trust them with power of which it could itself dictate the use to be made. Their power was but the nation's own power, concentrated and in a form convenient for exercise. This mode of thought, or rather perhaps of feeling, was common among the last generation of European liberalism, in the Continental section of which it still apparently predominates.[1] Those who admit any limit to what a government may do, except in the case of such governments as they think ought not to exist, stand out as brilliant exceptions among the political thinkers of the Continent. A similar tone of sentiment might by this time have been prevalent in our own country if the circumstances which for a time encouraged it had continued unaltered.

But, in political and philosophical theories as well as in persons, success discloses faults and infirmities which failure might have concealed from observation. The notion that the people have no need to limit their power over themselves might seem axiomatic, when popular government was a

---

1. This 'mode of thought' was even more common among the English utilitarians (the Philosophic Radicals). Indeed it was the main feature of their political philosophy. The very wording of this statement – the identification of rulers and ruled, the responsibility and removability of rulers, the concentrated exercise of power – could have been taken almost verbatim from Jeremy Bentham or James Mill. It may be that John Stuart Mill preferred to attribute these ideas to European or 'Continental' liberalism – the French enlightenment and its heirs – lest he seem to be criticizing (as he was) his own father.

thing only dreamed about, or read of as having existed at some distant period of the past. Neither was that notion necessarily disturbed by such temporary aberrations as those of the French Revolution, the worst of which were the work of a usurping few, and which, in any case, belonged, not to the permanent working of popular institutions, but to a sudden and convulsive outbreak against monarchical and aristocratic despotism. In time, however, a democratic republic came to occupy a large portion of the earth's surface and made itself felt as one of the most powerful members of the community of nations; and elective and responsible government became subject to the observations and criticisms which wait upon a great existing fact. It was now perceived that such phrases as 'self-government', and 'the power of the people over themselves', do not express the true state of the case. The 'people' who exercise the power are not always the same people with those over whom it is exercised; and the 'self-government' spoken of is not the government of each by himself, but of each by all the rest. The will of the people, moreover, practically means the will of the most numerous or the most active *part* of the people – the majority, or those who succeed in making themselves accepted as the majority; the people, consequently, *may* desire to oppress a part of their number, and precautions are as much needed against this as against any other abuse of power. The limitation, therefore, of the power of government over individuals loses none of its importance when the holders of power are regularly accountable to the community, that is, to the strongest party therein. This view of things, recommending itself equally to the intelligence of thinkers and to the inclination of those important classes in European society to whose real or supposed interests democracy is adverse, has had no difficulty in establishing itself; and in political speculations 'the tyranny of the majority' is now generally included among the evils against which society requires to be on its guard.[2]

2. This expression, or its variant 'despotism of the majority', was most prominently used by Alexis de Tocqueville in his *Democracy in America* (e.g., vol. I, ch. xv). Mill reviewed the first volume of Tocqueville's work

Like other tyrannies, the tyranny of the majority was at first, and is still vulgarly, held in dread, chiefly as operating through the acts of the public authorities. But reflecting persons perceived that when society is itself the tyrant – society collectively over the separate individuals who compose it – its means of tyrannizing are not restricted to the acts which it may do by the hands of its political functionaries. Society can and does execute its own mandates; and if it issues wrong mandates instead of right, or any mandates at all in things with which it ought not to meddle, it practises a social tyranny more formidable than many kinds of political oppression, since, though not usually upheld by such extreme penalties, it leaves fewer means of escape, penetrating much more deeply into the details of life, and enslaving the soul itself. Protection, therefore, against the tyranny of the magistrate is not enough; there needs protection also against the tyranny of the prevailing opinion and feeling, against the tendency of society to impose, by other means than civil penalties, its own ideas and practices as rules of conduct on those who dissent from them; to fetter the development and, if possible, prevent the formation of any individuality not in harmony with its ways, and compel all characters to fashion themselves upon the model of its own. There is a limit to the legitimate interference of collective opinion with individual independence; and to find that limit, and maintain it against encroachment, is as indispensable to a good condition of human affairs as protection against political despotism.

But though this proposition is not likely to be contested in general terms, the practical question where to place the limit – how to make the fitting adjustment between individual independence and social control – is a subject on which nearly everything remains to be done. All that makes existence valuable to anyone depends on the enforcement of restraints

in the *London and Westminster Review*, October 1835, and the second in the *Edinburgh Review*, October 1840. Only the second was reprinted in his *Dissertations and Discussions*, London, 1859, vol. II, pp. 1–83. Both are included in *Essays on Politics and Culture*; ed. Gertrude Himmelfarb, New York, 1962.

upon the actions of other people. Some rules of conduct, there-fore, must be imposed – by law in the first place, and by opinion on many things which are not fit subjects for the operation of law. What these rules should be is the principal question in human affairs; but if we except a few of the most obvious cases, it is one of those which least progress has been made in resolving. No two ages, and scarcely any two countries, have decided it alike; and the decision of one age or country is a wonder to another. Yet the people of any given age and coun-try no more suspect any difficulty in it than if it were a subject on which mankind had always been agreed. The rules which obtain among themselves appear to them self-evident and self-justifying. This all but universal illusion is one of the examples of the magical influence of custom, which is not only, as the proverb says, a second nature but is continually mistaken for the first. The effect of custom, in preventing any misgiving respecting the rules of conduct which mankind impose on one another, is all the more complete because the subject is one on which it is not generally considered necessary that reasons should be given, either by one person to others or by each to himself. People are accustomed to believe, and have been encouraged in the belief by some who aspire to the character of philosophers, that their feelings on subjects of this nature are better than reasons and render reasons unnecessary. The practical principle which guides them to their opinions on the regulation of human conduct is the feeling in each person's mind that everybody should be required to act as he, and those with whom he sympathizes, would like them to act. No one, indeed, acknowledges to himself that his standard of judgment is his own liking; but an opinion on a point of conduct, not supported by reasons, can only count as one person's prefer-ence; and if the reasons, when given, are a mere appeal to a similar preference felt by other people, it is still only many people's liking instead of one. To an ordinary man, however, his own preference, thus supported, is not only a perfectly satisfactory reason but the only one he generally has for any of his notions of morality, taste, or propriety, which are not expressly written in his religious creed, and his chief guide in the interpretation even of that. Men's opinions, accordingly, on what is laudable or blamable are affected by all the multifarious causes which influence their wishes in regard to the conduct of others, and which are as numerous as those which determine their wishes on any other subject. Sometimes their reason; at other times their prejudices or superstitions; often their social affections, not seldom their antisocial ones, their envy or jealousy, their arrogance or contemptuousness; but most commonly their desires or fears for themselves – their legitimate or illegitimate self-interest. Wherever there is an ascendant class, a large portion of the morality of the country emanates from its class interests and its feelings of class superiority. The morality between Spartans and Helots, between planters and Negroes, between princes and subjects, between nobles and roturiers,[3] between men and women has been for the most part the creation of these class interests and feelings; and the sentiments thus generated react in turn upon the moral feelings of the members of the ascendant class, in their relations among themselves. Where, on the other hand, a class, formerly ascendant, has lost its ascendancy, or where its ascendancy is unpopular, the prevailing moral sentiments frequently bear the impress of an impatient dislike of superiority. Another grand determining principle of the rules of conduct, both in act and forbearance, which have been enforced by law or opinion, has been the servility of mankind toward the supposed preferences or aversions of their temporal masters or of their gods. This servility, though essentially selfish, is not hypocrisy; it gives rise to perfectly genuine sentiments of abhorrence; it made men burn magicians and heretics. Among so many baser influences, the general and obvious interests of society have, of course, had a share, and a large one, in the direction of the moral sentiments; less, however, as a matter of reason, and on their own account, than as a consequence of the sympathies and antipathies which grew out of them; and sympathies and antipathies which had little or nothing to do with the interests of society have made themselves felt in the establishment of moralities with quite as great force.

3. Peasant farmers.

The likings and dislikings of society, or of some powerful portion of it, are thus the main thing which has practically determined the rules laid down for general observance, under the penalties of law or opinion. And in general, those who have been in advance of society in thought and feeling have left this condition of things unassailed in principle, however they may have come into conflict with it in some of its details. They have occupied themselves rather in inquiring what things society ought to like or dislike than in questioning whether its likings or dislikings should be a law to individuals. They preferred endeavouring to alter the feelings of mankind on the particular points on which they were themselves heretical rather than make common cause in defence of freedom with heretics generally. The only case in which the higher ground has been taken on principle and maintained with consistency, by any but an individual here and there, is that of religious belief: a case instructive in many ways, and not least so as forming a most striking instance of the fallibility of what is called the moral sense; for the *odium theologicum*,[4] in a sincere bigot, is one of the most unequivocal cases of moral feeling. Those who first broke the yoke of what called itself the Universal Church were in general as little willing to permit difference of religious opinion as that church itself. But when the heat of the conflict was over, without giving a complete victory to any party, and each church or sect was reduced to limit its hopes to retaining possession of the ground it already occupied, minorities, seeing that they had no chance of becoming majorities, were under the necessity of pleading to those whom they could not convert for permission to differ. It is accordingly on this battlefield, almost solely, that the rights of the individual against society have been asserted on broad grounds of principle, and the claim of society to exercise authority over dissentients openly controverted. The great writers to whom the world owes what religious liberty it possesses have mostly asserted freedom of conscience as an indefeasible right, and denied absolutely that a human being is

4. Theological hatred – i.e. the hostility engendered by religious differences.

accountable to others for his religious belief. Yet so natural to mankind is intolerance in whatever they really care about that religious freedom has hardly anywhere been practically realized, except where religious indifference, which dislikes to have its peace disturbed by theological quarrels, has added its weight to the scale. In the minds of almost all religious persons, even in the most tolerant countries, the duty of toleration is admitted with tacit reserves. One person will bear with dissent in matters of church government, but not of dogma; another can tolerate everybody, short of a Papist or a Unitarian; another, everyone who believes in revealed religion; a few extend their charity a little further, but stop at the belief in a God and in a future state. Wherever the sentiment of the majority is still genuine and intense, it is found to have abated little of its claim to be obeyed.

In England, from the peculiar circumstances of our political history, though the yoke of opinion is perhaps heavier, that of law is lighter than in most other countries of Europe; and there is considerable jealousy of direct interference by the legislative or the executive power with private conduct, not so much from any just regard for the independence of the individual as from the still subsisting habit of looking on the government as representing an opposite interest to the public. The majority have not yet learned to feel the power of the government their power, or its opinions their opinions. When they do so, individual liberty will probably be as much exposed to invasion from the government as it already is from public opinion. But, as yet, there is a considerable amount of feeling ready to be called forth against any attempt of the law to control individuals in things in which they have not hitherto been accustomed to be controlled by it; and this with very little discrimination as to whether the matter is, or is not, within the legitimate sphere of legal control; insomuch that the feeling, highly salutary on the whole, is perhaps quite as often misplaced as well grounded in the particular instances of its application. There is, in fact, no recognized principle by which the propriety or impropriety of government interference is customarily tested. People decide according to their personal preferences. Some, whenever they see any good to be done, or evil to be remedied, would willingly instigate the government to undertake the business, while others prefer to bear almost any amount of social evil rather than add one to the departments of human interests amenable to governmental control. And men range themselves on one or the other side in any particular case, according to this general direction of their sentiments, or according to the degree of interest which they feel in the particular thing which it is proposed that the government should do, or according to the belief they entertain that the government would, or would not, do it in the manner they prefer; but very rarely on account of any opinion to which they consistently adhere, as to what things are fit to be done by a government. And it seems to me that in consequence of this absence of rule or principle, one side is at present as often wrong as the other; the interference of government is, with about equal frequency, improperly invoked and improperly condemned.

The object of this essay is to assert one very simple principle, as entitled to govern absolutely the dealings of society with the individual in the way of compulsion and control, whether the means used be physical force in the form of legal penalties or the moral coercion of public opinion. That principle is that the sole end for which mankind are warranted, individually or collectively, in interfering with the liberty of action of any of their number is self-protection. That the only purpose for which power can be rightfully exercised over any member of a civilized community, against his will, is to prevent harm to others. His own good, either physical or moral, is not a sufficient warrant. He cannot rightfully be compelled to do or forbear because it will be better for him to do so, because it will make him happier, because, in the opinions of others, to do so would be wise or even right. These are good reasons for remonstrating with him, or reasoning with him, or persuading him, or entreating him, but not for compelling him or visiting him with any evil in case he do otherwise. To justify that, the conduct from which it is desired to deter him must be calculated to produce evil to someone else. The only part of the conduct of anyone for which he is amenable to society is that which concerns others. In the part which merely concerns himself, his independence is, of right, absolute. Over himself, over his own body and mind, the individual is sovereign.

It is, perhaps, hardly necessary to say that this doctrine is meant to apply only to human beings in the maturity of their faculties. We are not speaking of children or of young persons below the age which the law may fix as that of manhood or womanhood. Those who are still in a state to require being taken care of by others must be protected against their own actions as well as against external injury. For the same reason we may leave out of consideration those backward states of society in which the race itself may be considered as in its nonage. The early difficulties in the way of spontaneous progress are so great that there is seldom any choice of means for overcoming them; and a ruler full of the spirit of improvement is warranted in the use of any expedients that will attain an end perhaps otherwise unattainable. Despotism is a legitimate mode of government in dealing with barbarians, provided the end be their improvement and the means justified by actually effecting that end. Liberty, as a principle, has no application to any state of things anterior to the time when mankind have become capable of being improved by free and equal discussion. Until then, there is nothing for them but implicit obedience to an Akbar or a Charlemagne,[5] if they are so fortunate as to find one. But as soon as mankind have attained the capacity of being guided to their own improvement by conviction or persuasion (a period long since reached in all nations with whom we need here concern ourselves), compulsion, either in the direct form or in that of pains and penalties for noncompliance, is no longer admissible as a means to their own good, and justifiable only for the security of others.

It is proper to state that I forego any advantage which could be derived to my argument from the idea of abstract right as a

5. Akbar ('The Great') was the popular name of Jelal-ed-din-Moham-med (1542–1605), the Mogul emperor of India. Like Charlemagne (also 'The Great' – 742–814), he represents the type of empire builder who is also notable for his civilized and humane qualities.

thing independent of utility. I regard utility as the ultimate appeal on all ethical questions; but it must be utility in the largest sense, grounded on the permanent interests of man as a progressive being. Those interests, I contend, authorize the subjection of individual spontaneity to external control only in respect to those actions of each which concern the interest of other people. If anyone does an act hurtful to others, there is a *prima facie* case for punishing him by law or, where legal penalties are not safely applicable, by general disapprobation. There are also many positive acts for the benefit of others which he may rightfully be compelled to perform, such as to give evidence in a court of justice, to bear his fair share in the common defence or in any other joint work necessary to the interest of the society of which he enjoys the protection, and to perform certain acts of individual beneficence, such as saving a fellow creature's life or interposing to protect the defence-less against ill usage – things which whenever it is obviously a man's duty to do he may rightfully be made responsible to society for not doing. A person may cause evil to others not only by his actions but by his inaction, and in either case he is justly accountable to them for the injury. The latter case, it is true, requires a much more cautious exercise of compulsion than the former. To make anyone answerable for doing evil to others is the rule; to make him answerable for not preventing evil is, comparatively speaking, the exception. Yet there are many cases clear enough and grave enough to justify that exception. In all things which regard the external relations of the individual, he is *de jure* amenable to those whose interests are concerned, and, if need be, to society as their protector. There are often good reasons for not holding him to the responsibility; but these reasons must arise from the special expediencies of the case: either because it is a kind of case in which he is on the whole likely to act better when left to his own discretion than when controlled in any way in which society have it in their power to control him; or because the attempt to exercise control would produce other evils, greater than those which it would prevent. When such reasons as these preclude the enforcement of responsibility, the conscience of the agent himself should step into the vacant judgment seat and protect those interests of others which have no external protection; judging himself all the more rigidly, because the case does not admit of his being made accountable to the judgment of his fellow creatures.

But there is a sphere of action in which society, as distinguished from the individual, has, if any, only an indirect interest: comprehending all that portion of a person's life and conduct which affects only himself or, if it also affects others, only with their free, voluntary, and undeceived consent and participation. When I say only himself, I mean directly and in the first instance; for whatever affects himself may affect others through himself; and the objection which may be grounded on this contingency will receive consideration in the sequel. This, then, is the appropriate region of human liberty. It comprises, first, the inward domain of consciousness, demanding liberty of conscience in the most comprehensive sense, liberty of thought and feeling, absolute freedom of opinion and sentiment on all subjects, practical or speculative, scientific, moral, or theological. The liberty of expressing and publishing opinions may seem to fall under a different principle, since it belongs to that part of the conduct of an individual which concerns other people, but, being almost of as much importance as the liberty of thought itself and resting in great part on the same reasons, is practically inseparable from it. Secondly, the principle requires liberty of tastes and pursuits, of framing the plan of our life to suit our own character, of doing as we like, subject to such consequences as may follow, without impediment from our fellow creatures, so long as what we do does not harm them, even though they should think our conduct foolish, perverse, or wrong. Thirdly, from this liberty of each individual follows the liberty, within the same limits, of combination among individuals; freedom to unite for any purpose not involving harm to others: the persons combining being supposed to be of full age and not forced or deceived.

No society in which these liberties are not, on the whole, respected is free, whatever may be its form of government; and none is completely free in which they do not exist absolute and unqualified. The only freedom which deserves the name is that of pursuing our own good in our own way, so long as we do not attempt to deprive others of theirs or impede their efforts to obtain it. Each is the proper guardian of his own health, whether bodily *or* mental and spiritual. Mankind are greater gainers by suffering each other to live as seems good to themselves than by compelling each to live as seems good to the rest.

Though this doctrine is anything but new and, to some persons, may have the air of a truism, there is no doctrine which stands more directly opposed to the general tendency of existing opinion and practice. Society has expended fully as much effort in the attempt (according to its lights) to compel people to conform to its notions of personal as of social excellence. The ancient commonwealths thought themselves entitled to practise, and the ancient philosophers countenanced, the regulation of every part of private conduct by public authority, on the ground that the State had a deep interest in the whole bodily and mental discipline of every one of its citizens – a mode of thinking which may have been admissible in small republics surrounded by powerful enemies, in constant peril of being subverted by foreign attack or internal commotion, and to which even a short interval of relaxed energy and self-command might so easily be fatal that they could not afford to wait for the salutary permanent effects of freedom. In the modern world, the greater size of political communities and, above all, the separation between spiritual and temporal authority (which placed the direction of men's consciences in other hands than those which controlled their worldly affairs) prevented so great an interference by law in the details of private life; but the engines of moral repression have been wielded more strenuously against divergence from the reigning opinion in self-regarding than even in social matters; religion, the most powerful of the elements which have entered into the formation of moral feeling, having almost always been governed either by the ambition of a hierarchy seeking control over every department of human conduct, or by the spirit of Puritanism. And some of those modern reformers who have placed themselves in strongest opposition to the religions of the past have been noway behind either churches or sects in their assertion of the right of spiritual domination: M. Comte, in particular, whose social system, as unfolded in his *Système de Politique Positive*, aims at establishing (though by moral more than by legal appliances) a despotism of society over the individual surpassing anything contemplated in the political ideal of the most rigid disciplinarian among the ancient philosophers.[6]

Apart from the peculiar tenets of individual thinkers, there is also in the world at large an increasing inclination to stretch unduly the powers of society over the individual both by the force of opinion and even by that of legislation; and as the tendency of all the changes taking place in the world is to strengthen society and diminish the power of the individual, this encroachment is not one of the evils which tend spontaneously to disappear, but, on the contrary, to grow more and more formidable. The disposition of mankind, whether as rulers or as fellow citizens, to impose their own opinions and inclinations as a rule of conduct on others is so energetically supported by some of the best and by some of the worst feelings incident to human nature that it is hardly ever kept under restraint by anything but want of power; and as the power is not declining, but growing, unless a strong barrier of

6. Mill had once been more favourably disposed to Auguste Comte (1798-1857). Comte's earlier work, the six-volume *Cours de Philosophie Positive* (1830-42), had led to a long correspondence between them and had much influenced parts of Mill's *System of Logic*. (In later editions of the *Logic*, Mill minimized that influence.) Although Mill continued to respect Comte's efforts to create a 'science of society' and remained impressed with his idea of a 'Religion of Humanity', he became increasingly disturbed by the later direction of Comte's thought: first by his views on women (Comte regarded women as significantly different from men intellectually and morally as well as physically), and then by the highly organized, extremely rigid social and religious system elaborated in the *Système de Politique Positive* (1851-54). After Comte has lost his position at the École Polytechnique, Mill raised funds among his friends for Comte's support. When those contributions ceased, Comte held Mill personally responsible and complained bitterly to him, an episode that further estranged the two men.

moral conviction can be raised against the mischief, we must expect, in the present circumstances of the world, to see it increase.

It will be convenient for the argument if, instead of at once entering upon the general thesis, we confine ourselves in the first instance to a single branch of it on which the principle here stated is, if not fully, yet to a certain point, recognized by the current opinions. This one branch is the Liberty of Thought, from which it is impossible to separate the cognate liberty of speaking and of writing. Although these liberties, to some considerable amount, form part of the political morality of all countries which profess religious toleration and free institutions, the grounds, both philosophical and practical, on which they rest are perhaps not so familiar to the general mind, nor so thoroughly appreciated by many, even of the leaders of opinion, as might have been expected. Those grounds, when rightly understood, are of much wider application than to only one division of the subject, and a thorough consideration of this part of the question will be found the best introduction to the remainder. Those to whom nothing I am about to say will be new may therefore, I hope, excuse me if on a subject which for now three centuries has been so often discussed I venture on one discussion more.

CHAPTER II

Of the Liberty of
Thought and Discussion

THE time, it is to be hoped, is gone by when any defence would be necessary of the 'liberty of the press' as one of the securities against corrupt or tyrannical government. No argument, we may suppose, can now be needed against permitting a legislature or an executive, not identified in interest with the people, to prescribe opinions to them and determine what doctrines or what arguments they shall be allowed to hear. This aspect of the question, besides, has been so often and so triumphantly enforced by preceding writers that it needs not be specially insisted on in this place. Though the law of England, on the subject of the press, is as servile to this day as it was in the time of the Tudors, there is little danger of its being actually put in force against political discussion except during some temporary panic when fear of insurrection drives ministers and judges from their propriety;* and, speaking

---

* These words had scarcely been written when, as if to give them an emphatic contradiction, occurred the Government Press Prosecutions of 1858. That ill-judged interference with the liberty of public discussion has not, however, induced me to alter a single word in the text, nor has it at all weakened my conviction that, moments of panic excepted, the era of pains and penalties for political discussion has, in our own country, passed away. For, in the first place, the prosecutions were not persisted in; and, in the second, they were never, properly speaking, political prosecutions. The offence charged was not that of criticizing institutions or the acts or persons of rulers, but of circulating what was deemed an immoral doctrine, the lawfulness of tyrannicide.

If the arguments of the present chapter are of any validity, there ought to exist the fullest liberty of professing and discussing, as a matter of ethical conviction, any doctrine, however immoral it may be considered. It would, therefore, be irrelevant and out of place to examine here whether the doctrine of tyrannicide deserves that title. I shall content myself with saying that the subject has been at all times one of the open questions of morals; that the act of a private citizen in striking down a criminal who, by raising himself above the law, has placed himself beyond the reach of legal punishment or control has been accounted by whole nations, and by generally, it is not, in constitutional countries, to be apprehended that the government, whether completely responsible to the people or not, will often attempt to control the expression of opinion, except when in doing so it makes itself the organ of the general intolerance of the public. Let us suppose, therefore, that the government is entirely at one with the people, and never thinks of exerting any power of coercion unless in agreement with what it conceives to be their voice. But I deny the right of the people to exercise such coercion, either by themselves or by their government. The power itself is illegitimate. The best government has no more title to it than the worst. It is as noxious, or more noxious, when exerted in accordance with public opinion than when in opposition to it. If all mankind minus one were of one opinion, mankind would be no more justified in silencing that one person than he, if he had the power, would be justified in silencing mankind. Were an opinion a personal possession of no value except to the owner, if to be obstructed in the enjoyment of it were simply a private injury, it would make some difference whether the injury was inflicted only on a few persons or on many. But the peculiar evil of silencing the expression of an opinion is that it is robbing the human race, posterity as well as the existing generation – those who dissent from the opinion, still more than those who hold it. If the opinion is right, they are deprived of the opportunity of exchanging error for truth; if wrong, they lose, what is almost as great a benefit, the clearer perception and livelier impression of truth produced by its collision with error.

It is necessary to consider separately these two hypotheses, each of which has a distinct branch of the argument corresponding to it. We can never be sure that the opinion we are

---

some of the best and wisest of men, not a crime but an act of exalted virtue; and that, right or wrong, it is not of the nature of assassination, but of civil war. As such, I hold that the instigation to it, in a specific case, may be a proper subject of punishment, but only if an overt act has followed, and at least a probable connection can be established between the act and the instigation. Even then it is not a foreign government but the very government assailed which alone, in the exercise of self-defence, can legitimately punish attacks directed against its own existence.

endeavouring to stifle is a false opinion; and if we were sure, stifling it would be an evil still.

First, the opinion which it is attempted to suppress by authority may possibly be true. Those who desire to suppress if, of course, deny its truth; but they are not infallible. They have no authority to decide the question for all mankind and exclude every other person from the means of judging. To refuse a hearing to an opinion because they are sure that it is false is to assume that *their* certainty is the same thing as *absolute* certainty. All silencing of discussion is an assumption of infallibility. Its condemnation may be allowed to rest on this common argument, not the worse for being common.

Unfortunately for the good sense of mankind, the fact of their fallibility is far from carrying the weight in their practical judgement which is always allowed to it in theory; for while everyone well knows himself to be fallible, few think it necessary to take any precautions against their own fallibility, or admit the supposition that any opinion of which they feel very certain may be one of the examples of the error to which they acknowledge themselves to be liable. Absolute princes, or others who are accustomed to unlimited deference, usually feel this complete confidence in their own opinions on nearly all subjects. People more happily situated, who sometimes hear their opinions disputed and are not wholly unused to be set right when they are wrong, place the same unbounded reliance only on such of their opinions as are shared by all who surround them, or to whom they habitually defer; for in proportion to a man's want of confidence in his own solitary judgement does he usually repose, with implicit trust, on the infallibility of 'the world' in general. And the world, to each individual, means the part of it with which he comes in contact: his party, his sect, his church, his class of society; the man may be called, by comparison, almost liberal and large-minded to whom it means anything so comprehensive as his own country or his own age. Nor is his own faith in this collective authority at all shaken by his being aware that other ages, countries, sects, churches, classes, and parties have thought, and even now think, the exact reverse. He devolves upon his own world the responsibility of being in the right against the dissentient worlds of other people; and it never troubles him that mere accident has decided which of these numerous worlds is the object of his reliance, and that the same causes which make him a churchman in London would have made him a Buddhist or a Confucian in Peking. Yet it is as evident in itself, as any amount of argument can make it, that ages are no more infallible than individuals – every age having held many opinions which subsequent ages have deemed not only false but absurd; and it is as certain that many opinions, now general, will be rejected by future ages, as it is that many, once general, are rejected by the present.

The objection likely to be made to this argument would probably take some such form as the following. There is no greater assumption of infallibility in forbidding the propagation of error than in any other thing which is done by public authority on its own judgement and responsibility. Judgement is given to men that they may use it. Because it may be used erroneously, are men to be told that they ought not to use it at all? To prohibit what they think pernicious is not claiming exemption from error, but fulfilling the duty incumbent on them, although fallible, of acting on their conscientious conviction. If we were never to act on our opinions, because those opinions may be wrong, we should leave all our interests uncared for, and all our duties unperformed. An objection which applies to all conduct can be no valid objection to any conduct in particular. It is the duty of governments, and of individuals, to form the truest opinions they can; to form them carefully, and never impose them upon others unless they are quite sure of being right. But when they are sure (such reasoners may say), it is not conscientiousness but cowardice to shrink from acting on their opinions and allow doctrines which they honestly think dangerous to the welfare of mankind, either in this life or in another, to be scattered abroad without restraint, because other people, in less enlightened times, have persecuted opinions now believed to be true. Let us take care, it may be said, not to make the same mistake; but governments and nations have made mistakes in other things which are not denied to be fit subjects for the exercise of authority: they have laid on bad taxes, made unjust wars. Ought we therefore to lay on no taxes and, under whatever provocation, make no wars? Men and governments must act to the best of their ability. There is no such thing as absolute certainty, but there is assurance sufficient for the purposes of human life. We may, and must, assume our opinion to be true for the guidance of our own conduct; and it is assuming no more when we forbid bad men to pervert society by the propagation of opinions which we regard as false and pernicious.

I answer, that it is assuming very much more. There is the greatest difference between presuming an opinion to be true because, with every opportunity for contesting it, it has not been refuted, and assuming its truth for the purpose of not permitting its refutation. Complete liberty of contradicting and disproving our opinion is the very condition which justifies us in assuming its truth for purposes of action; and on no other terms can a being with human faculties have any rational assurance of being right.

When we consider either the history of opinion or the ordinary conduct of human life, to what is it to be ascribed that the one and the other are no worse than they are? Not certainly to the inherent force of the human understanding, for on any matter not self-evident there are ninety-nine persons totally incapable of judging of it for one who is capable; and the capacity of the hundredth person is only comparative, for the majority of the eminent men of every past generation held many opinions now known to be erroneous, and did or approved numerous things which no one will now justify. Why is it, then, that there is on the whole a preponderance among mankind of rational opinions and rational conduct? If there really is this preponderance – which there must be unless human affairs are, and have always been, in an almost desperate state – it is owing to a quality of the human mind, the source of everything respectable in man either as an intellectual or as a moral being, namely, that his errors are corrigible. He is capable of rectifying his mistakes by discussion and experience. Not by experience alone. There must be discussion to show how experience is to be interpreted. Wrong opinions and practices gradually yield to fact and argument; but facts and arguments, to produce any effect on the mind, must be brought before it. Very few facts are able to tell their own story, without comments to bring out their meaning. The whole strength and value, then, of human judgement depending on the one property, that it can be set right when it is wrong, reliance can be placed on it only when the means of setting it right are kept constantly at hand. In the case of any person whose judgement is really deserving of confidence, how has it become so? Because he has kept his mind open to criticism of his opinions and conduct. Because it has been his practice to listen to all that could be said against him; to profit by as much of it as was just, and to expound to himself, and upon occasion to others, the fallacy of what was fallacious. Because he has felt that the only way in which a human being can make some approach to knowing the whole of a subject is by hearing what can be said about it by persons of every variety of opinion, and studying all modes in which it can be looked at by every character of mind. No wise man ever acquired his wisdom in any mode but this; nor is it in the nature of human intellect to become wise in any other manner. The steady habit of correcting and completing his own opinion by collating it with those of others, so far from causing doubt and hesitation in carrying it into practice, is the only stable foundation for a just reliance on it; for, being cognizant of all that can, at least obviously, be said against him, and having taken up his position against all gainsayers – knowing that he has sought for objections and difficulties instead of avoiding them, and has shut out no light which can be thrown upon the subject from any quarter – he has a right to think his judgement better than that of any person, or any multitude, who have not gone through a similar process.

It is not too much to require that what the wisest of mankind, those who are best entitled to trust their own judgement, find necessary to warrant their relying on it, should be submitted to by that miscellaneous collection of a few wise and many foolish individuals called the public. The most intolerant of churches, the Roman Catholic Church, even at the canonization of a saint admits, and listens patiently to, a 'devil's advocate'. The holiest of men, it appears, cannot be admitted to posthumous honours until all that the devil could say against him is known and weighed. If even the Newtonian philosophy were not permitted to be questioned, mankind could not feel as complete assurance of its truth as they now do. The beliefs which we have most warrant for have no safeguard to rest on but a standing invitation to the whole world to prove them unfounded. If the challenge is not accepted, or is accepted and the attempt fails, we are far enough from certainty still, but we have done the best that the existing state of human reason admits of: we have neglected nothing that could give the truth a chance of reaching us; if the lists are kept open, we may hope that, if there be a better truth, it will be found when the human mind is capable of receiving it; and in the meantime we may rely on having attained such approach to truth as is possible in our own day. This is the amount of certainty attainable by a fallible being, and this the sole way of attaining it.

Strange it is that men should admit the validity of the arguments for free discussion, but object to their being 'pushed to an extreme', not seeing that unless the reasons are good for an extreme case, they are not good for any case. Strange that they should imagine that they are not assuming infallibility when they acknowledge that there should be free discussion on all subjects which can possibly be *doubtful*, but think that some particular principle or doctrine should be forbidden to be questioned because it is so *certain*, that is, because *they are certain* that it is certain. To call any proposition certain, while there is anyone who would deny its certainty if permitted, but who is not permitted, is to assume that we ourselves, and those who agree with us, are the judges of certainty, and judges without hearing the other side.

In the present age – which has been described as 'destitute

of faith, but terrified at scepticism'[7] – in which people feel sure, not so much that their opinions are true as that they should not know what to do without them – the claims of an opinion to be protected from public attack are rested not so much on its truth as on its importance to society. There are, it is alleged, certain beliefs so useful, not to say indispensable, to well-being that it is as much the duty of governments to uphold those beliefs as to protect any other of the interests of society. In a case of such necessity, and so directly in the line of their duty, something less than infallibility may, it is maintained, warrant, and even bind, governments to act on their own opinion confirmed by the general opinion of mankind. It is also often argued, and still oftener thought, that none but bad men would desire to weaken these salutary beliefs; and there can be nothing wrong, it is thought, in restraining bad men and prohibiting what only such men would wish to practise. This mode of thinking makes the justification of restraints on discussion not a question of the truth of doctrines but of their usefulness, and flatters itself by that means to escape the responsibility of claiming to be an infallible judge of opinions. But those who thus satisfy themselves do not perceive that the assumption of infallibility is merely shifted from one point to another. The usefulness of an opinion is itself matter of opinion – as disputable, as open to discussion, and requiring discussion as much as the opinion itself. There is the same need of an infallible judge of opinions to decide an opinion to be noxious as to decide it to be false, unless the opinion condemned has full opportunity of defending itself. And it will not do to say that the heretic may be allowed to maintain the utility or harmlessness of his opinion, though forbidden to maintain its truth. The truth of an opinion is part of its utility. If we would know whether or not it is desirable that a proposition should be believed, is it possible to exclude the consideration of whether or not it is true? In the opinion, not of bad men, but of the best men, no belief

7. This expression (with 'and' in place of 'but') was used by Thomas Carlyle in his essay on Sir Walter Scott. (Carlyle, *Critical and Miscellaneous Essays*, 7 vols.; London, 1869, vol. VI, p. 46.

which is contrary to truth can be really useful; and can you prevent such men from urging that plea when they are charged with culpability for denying some doctrine which they are told is useful, but which they believe to be false? Those who are on the side of received opinions never fail to take all possible advantage of this plea; you do not find *them* handling the question of utility as if it could be completely abstracted from that of truth; on the contrary, it is, above all, because their doctrine is 'the truth' that the knowledge or the belief of it is held to be so indispensable. There can be no fair discussion of the question of usefulness when an argument so vital may be employed on one side, but not on the other. And in point of fact, when law or public feeling do not permit the truth of an opinion to be disputed, they are just as little tolerant of a denial of its usefulness. The utmost they allow is an extenuation of its absolute necessity, or of the positive guilt of rejecting it.

In order more fully to illustrate the mischief of denying a hearing to opinions because we, in our own judgement, have condemned them, it will be desirable to fix down the discussion to a concrete case: and I choose, by preference, the cases which are least favourable to me – in which the argument against freedom of opinion, both on the score of truth and on that of utility, is considered the strongest. Let the opinions impugned be the belief in a God and in a future state, or any of the commonly received doctrines of morality. To fight the battle on such ground gives a great advantage to an unfair antagonist, since he will be sure to say (and many who have no desire to be unfair will say it internally), Are these the doctrines which you do not deem sufficiently certain to be taken under the protection of law? Is the belief in a God one of the opinions to feel sure of which you hold to be assuming infallibility? But I must be permitted to observe that it is not the feeling sure of a doctrine (be it what it may) which I call an assumption of infallibility. It is the undertaking to decide that question *for others*, without allowing them to hear what can be said on the contrary side. And I denounce and reprobate this pretension not the less if put forth on the side of my most solemn convictions. However positive anyone's persuasion may be, not only of the falsity but of the pernicious consequences – not only of the pernicious consequences, but (to adopt expressions which I altogether condemn) the immorality and impiety of an opinion – yet if, in pursuance of that private judgement, though backed by the public judgement of his country or his contemporaries, he prevents the opinion from being heard in its defence, he assumes infallibility. And so far from the assumption being less objectionable or less dangerous because the opinion is called immoral or impious, this is the case of all others in which it is most fatal. These are exactly the occasions on which the men of one generation commit those dreadful mistakes which excite the astonishment and horror of posterity. It is among such that we find the instances memorable in history, when the arm of the law has been employed to root out the best men and the noblest doctrines; with deplorable success as to the men, though some of the doctrines have survived to be (as if in mockery) invoked in defence of similar conduct towards those who dissent from *them*, or from their received interpretation.

Mankind can hardly be too often reminded that there was once a man called Socrates, between whom and the legal authorities and public opinion of his time there took place a memorable collision. Born in an age and country abounding in individual greatness, this man has been handed down to us by those who best knew both him and the age, as the most virtuous man in it; while *we* know him as the head and prototype of all subsequent teachers of virtue, the source equally of the lofty inspiration of Plato and the judicious utilitarianism of Aristotle, '*i maëstri di color che sanno*',[8] the two headsprings of ethical as of all other philosophy. This acknowledged master of all the eminent thinkers who have since lived – whose fame, still growing after more than two thousand years, all but outweighs the whole remainder of the names which make his native city illustrious – was put to death by his countrymen,

8. Dante's phrase, in the singular, was a reference to Aristotle: 'the master of those who know'. Mill pluralized it ('the masters . . .') to refer to both Plato and Aristotle.

after a judicial conviction, for impiety and immorality. Impiety, in denying the gods recognized by the State; indeed, his accuser asserted (see the *Apologia*) that he believed in no gods at all. Immorality, in being, by his doctrines and instructions, a 'corruptor of youth'. Of these charges the tribunal, there is every ground for believing, honestly found him guilty, and condemned the man who probably of all then born had deserved least of mankind to be put to death as a criminal.

To pass from this to the only other instance of judicial iniquity, the mention of which, after the condemnation of Socrates, would not be an anticlimax: the event which took place on Calvary rather more than eighteen hundred years ago. The man who left on the memory of those who witnessed his life and conversation such an impression of his moral grandeur that eighteen subsequent centuries have done homage to him as the Almighty in person, was ignominiously put to death, as what? As a blasphemer. Men did not merely mistake their benefactor, they mistook him for the exact contrary of what he was and treated him as that prodigy of impiety which they themselves are now held to be for their treatment of him. The feelings with which mankind now regard these lamentable transactions, especially the latter of the two, render them extremely unjust in their judgement of the unhappy actors. These were, to all appearance, not bad men – not worse than men commonly are, but rather the contrary; men who possessed in a full, or somewhat more than a full measure, the religious, moral, and patriotic feelings of their time and people: the very kind of men who, in all times, our own included, have every chance of passing through life blameless and respected. The high priest who rent his garments when the words were pronounced, which, according to all the ideas of his country, constituted the blackest guilt, was in all probability quite as sincere in his horror and indignation as the generality of respectable and pious men now are in the religious and moral sentiments they profess; and most of those who now shudder at his conduct, if they had lived in his time, and been born Jews, would have acted precisely as he did. Orthodox Christians who are tempted to think that those who stoned to death

the first martyrs must have been worse men than they themselves are ought to remember that one of those persecutors was
Saint Paul.

Let us add one more example, the most striking of all, if
the impressiveness of an error is measured by the wisdom and
virtue of him who falls into it. If ever anyone possessed of power
had grounds for thinking himself the best and most enlightened among his contemporaries, it was the Emperor Marcus
Aurelius.[9] Absolute monarch of the whole civilized world, he
preserved through life not only the most unblemished justice,
but what was less to be expected from his Stoical breeding, the
tenderest heart. The few failings which are attributed to him
were all on the side of indulgence, while his writings, the
highest ethical product of the ancient mind, differ scarcely
perceptibly, if they differ at all, from the most characteristic
teachings of Christ. This man, a better Christian in all but the
dogmatic sense of the word than almost any of the ostensibly
Christian sovereigns who have since reigned, persecuted
Christianity. Placed at the summit of all the previous attainments of humanity, with an open, unfettered intellect, and a
character which led him of himself to embody in his moral
writings the Christian ideal, he yet failed to see that Christianity
was to be a good and not an evil to the world, with his duties
to which he was so deeply penetrated. Existing society he
knew to be in a deplorable state. But such as it was, he saw, or
thought he saw, that it was held together, and prevented from
being worse, by belief and reverence of the received divinities.
As a ruler of mankind, he deemed it his duty not to suffer
society to fall in pieces; and saw not how, if its existing ties
were removed, any others could be formed which could
again knit it together. The new religion openly aimed at
dissolving these ties; unless, therefore, it was his duty to
adopt that religion, it seemed to be his duty to put it down.
Inasmuch then as the theology of Christianity did not appear

9. Marcus Aurelius Antoninus (121–180). It was in his essay on Marcus
Aurelius that Matthew Arnold cited Mill's views on Christianity and
paganism. (Arnold, *Lectures and Essays in Criticism*, ed. R. H. Super, [Ann
Arbor, 1962], p. 133.)

to him true or of divine origin, inasmuch as this strange history of a crucified God was not credible to him, and a system which purported to rest entirely upon a foundation to him so wholly unbelievable, could not be foreseen by him to be that renovating agency which, after all abatements, it has in fact proved to be; the gentlest and most amiable of philosophers and rulers, under a solemn sense of duty, authorized the persecution of Christianity. To my mind this is one of the most tragical facts in all history. It is a bitter thought how different a thing the Christianity of the world might have been if the Christian faith had been adopted as the religion of the empire under the auspices of Marcus Aurelius instead of those of Constantine. But it would be equally unjust to him and false to truth to deny that no one plea which can be urged for punishing anti-Christian teaching was wanting to Marcus Aurelius for punishing, as he did, the propagation of Christianity. No Christian more firmly believes that atheism is false and tends to the dissolution of society than Marcus Aurelius believed the same things of Christianity; he who, of all men then living, might have been thought the most capable of appreciating it. Unless anyone who approves of punishment for the promulgation of opinions flatters himself that he is a wiser and better man than Marcus Aurelius – more deeply versed in the wisdom of his time, more elevated in his intellect above it, more earnest in his search for truth, or more single-minded in his devotion to it when found – let him abstain from that assumption of the joint infallibility of himself and the multitude which the great Antoninus made with so unfortunate a result.

Aware of the impossibility of defending the use of punishment for restraining irreligious opinions by any argument which will not justify Marcus Antoninus, the enemies of religious freedom, when hard pressed, occasionally accept this consequence and say, with Dr Johnson, that the persecutors of Christianity were in the right, that persecution is an ordeal through which truth ought to pass, and always passes successfully, legal penalties being, in the end, powerless against truth, though, sometimes beneficially effective against mischievous errors.[10] This is a form of the argument for religious intolerance sufficiently remarkable not to be passed without notice.

A theory which maintains that truth may justifiably be persecuted because persecution cannot possibly do it any harm cannot be charged with being intentionally hostile to the reception of new truths; but we cannot commend the generosity of its dealing with the persons to whom mankind are indebted for them. To discover to the world something which deeply concerns it, and of which it was previously ignorant, to prove to it that it had been mistaken on some vital point of temporal or spiritual interest, is as important a service as a human being can render to his fellow creatures, and in certain cases, as in those of the early Christians and of the Reformers, those who think with Dr Johnson believe it to have been the most precious gift which could be bestowed on mankind. That the authors of such splendid benefits should be requited by martyrdom, that their reward should be to be dealt with as the vilest of criminals, is not, upon this theory, a deplorable error and misfortune for which humanity should mourn in sackcloth and ashes, but the normal and justifiable state of things. The propounder of a new truth, according to this doctrine, should stand, as stood, in the legislation of the Locrians,[11] the proposer of a new law, with a halter round his neck, to be instantly tightened if the public assembly did not, on hearing his reasons, then and there adopt his proposition. People who defend this mode of treating benefactors cannot be supposed to set much value on the benefit; and I believe this view of the subject is mostly confined to the sort of persons who

10. Samuel Johnson: 'The only method by which religious truth can be established is by martyrdom. The magistrate has a right to enforce what he thinks; and he who is conscious of the truth has a right to suffer. I am afraid there is no other way of ascertaining the truth, but by persecution on the one hand and enduring it on the other.' *Life of Johnson*, by James Boswell, ed. George Birkbeck Hill and Rev. L. F. Powell, 6 vols.; Oxford, 1971, vol. II, p. 250 (7 May 1773). See also vol. IV, p. 12 (1780).

11. The Locrian legal code, generally attributed to Zaleucus (7th century B.C.), was the earliest written code in Europe. It was also, as Mill's example suggests, famous for its severity.

think that new truths may have been desirable once, but that we have had enough of them now.

But, indeed, the dictum that truth always triumphs over persecution is one of those pleasant falsehoods which men repeat after one another till they pass into commonplaces, but which all experience refutes. History teems with instances of truth put down by persecution. If not suppressed forever, it may be thrown back for centuries. To speak only of religious opinions: the Reformation broke out at least twenty times before Luther, and was put down. Arnold of Brescia was put down. Fra Dolcino was put down. Savonarola was put down. The Albigeois were put down. The Vaudois were put down. The Lollards were put down. The Hussites were put down.[12] Even after the era of Luther, wherever persecution was

---

12. Arnold of Brescia, involved in an insurrection against the papal government in Rome, was defeated and executed in 1155.

Fra Dolcino was the head of a sect of 'Apostles' and author of a famous epistle declaring the Pope to be anti-Christ. Four crusades against it were waged before the sect was finally decimated. Dolcino himself was publicly tortured to death in 1307.

The famous preacher and reformer, Girolamo Savonarola, whose religious zeal also involved him in political opposition to the Medici, was found guilty of heresy and executed in 1498.

The Albigeois (more commonly known as the Albigensians) adhered to such heretical doctrines as the Manichean duality of good and evil and the Gnostic denial of the bodily reality of Jesus. A crusade against them was proclaimed by Pope Innocent III in 1208, and the legal proceedings initiated by Pope Gregory IX in 1233 are generally taken to mark the beginning of the Inquisition.

The Vaudois (more often referred to as the Waldenses or Waldensians) affirmed the Bible as the sole rule of life and faith. The sect was declared heretical in 1215 but continued to flourish and eventually merged with the Reformed Church in 1532. They were not quite 'put down', as Mill says; indeed in 1848 King Charles Albert of Savoy granted them full political and religious rights.

The Lollards, an English sect of the late 14th century led by John Wyclif, also proclaimed the Bible as the only true source of faith. In spite of severe persecutions, it survived underground until the 16th century.

The Hussites adhered to most of Wyclif's doctrines. John Huss, burned at the stake in 1415, became both a religious martyr and a national hero of Czechoslovakia. After his death one branch of the sect became famous for its advocacy of a form of primitive communism.

89

persisted in, it was successful. In Spain, Italy, Flanders, the Austrian empire, Protestantism was rooted out; and, most likely, would have been so in England had Queen Mary lived or Queen Elizabeth died. Persecution has always succeeded save where the heretics were too strong a party to be effectually persecuted. No reasonable person can doubt that Christianity might have been extirpated in the Roman Empire. It spread and became predominant because the persecutions were only occasional, lasting but a short time, and separated by long intervals of almost undisturbed propagandism. It is a piece of idle sentimentality that truth, merely as truth, has any inherent power denied to error of prevailing against the dungeon and the stake. Men are not more zealous for truth than they often are for error, and a sufficient application of legal or even of social penalties will generally succeed in stopping the propagation of either. The real advantage which truth has consists in this, that when an opinion is true, it may be extinguished once, twice, or many times, but in the course of ages there will generally be found persons to rediscover it, until some one of its reappearances falls on a time when from favourable circumstances it escapes persecution until it has made such head as to withstand all subsequent attempts to suppress it.

It will be said that we do not now put to death the introducers of new opinions: we are not like our fathers who slew the prophets; we even build sepulchres to them. It is true we no longer put heretics to death; and the amount of penal infliction which modern feeling would probably tolerate, even against the most obnoxious opinions, is not sufficient to extirpate them. But let us not flatter ourselves that we are yet free from the stain even of legal persecution. Penalties for opinion, or at least for its expression, still exist by law; and their enforcement is not, even in these times, so unexampled as to make it at all incredible that they may some day be revived in full force. In the year 1857, at the summer assizes of the county of Cornwall, an unfortunate man, said to be of unexceptionable conduct in all relations of life, was sentenced to twenty-one months' imprisonment for uttering, and writing

on a gate, some offensive words concerning Christianity.*
Within a month of the same time, at the Old Bailey, two persons, on two separate occasions,† were rejected as jurymen,
and one of them grossly insulted by the judge and by one of
the counsel, because they honestly declared that they had no
theological belief; and a third, a foreigner,‡ for the same reason,
was denied justice against a thief. This refusal of redress took
place in virtue of the legal doctrine that no person can be
allowed to give evidence in a court of justice who does not
profess belief in a God (any god is sufficient) and in a future
state, which is equivalent to declaring such persons to be
outlaws, excluded from the protection of the tribunals; who
may not only be robbed or assaulted with impunity, if no one
but themselves, or persons of similar opinions, be present, but
anyone else may be robbed or assaulted with impunity if the
proof of the fact depends on their evidence. The assumption
on which this is grounded is that the oath is worthless of a
person who does not believe in a future state – a proposition
which betokens much ignorance of history in those who assent
to it (since it is historically true that a large proportion of
infidels in all ages have been persons of distinguished integrity
and honour), and would be maintained by no one who had
the smallest conception how many of the persons in greatest
repute with the world, both for virtues and attainments, are
well known, at least to their intimates, to be unbelievers. The
rule, besides, is suicidal and cuts away its own foundation.
Under pretence that atheists must be liars, it admits the testimony of all atheists who are willing to lie, and rejects only
those who brave the obloquy of publicly confessing a detested
creed rather than affirm a falsehood. A rule thus self-convicted
of absurdity so far as regards its professed purpose can be kept
in force only as a badge of hatred, a relic of persecution – a

* Thomas Pooley, Bodmin Assizes, July 31, 1857. In December following, he received a free pardon from the Crown.
† George Jacob Holyoake, August 17, 1857; Edward Truelove, July,
1857.
‡ Baron de Gleichen, Marlborough Street Police Court, August 4,
1857.

persecution, too, having the peculiarity that the qualification for undergoing it is the being clearly proved not to deserve it. The rule and the theory it implies are hardly less insulting to believers than to infidels. For if he who does not believe in a future state necessarily lies, it follows that they who do believe are only prevented from lying, if prevented they are, by the fear of hell. We will not do the authors and abettors of the rule the injury of supposing that the conception which they have formed of Christian virtue is drawn from their own consciousness.

These, indeed, are but rags and remnants of persecution, and may be thought to be not so much an indication of the wish to persecute, as an example of that very frequent infirmity of English minds, which makes them take a preposterous pleasure in the assertion of a bad principle, when they are no longer bad enough to desire to carry it really into practice. But unhappily there is no security in the state of the public mind that the suspension of worse forms of legal persecution, which has lasted for about the space of a generation, will continue. In this age the quiet surface of routine is as often ruffled by attempts to resuscitate past evils as to introduce new benefits. What is boasted of at the present time as the revival of religion is always, in narrow and uncultivated minds, at least as much the revival of bigotry; and where there is the strong permanent leaven of intolerance in the feelings of a people, which at all times abides in the middle classes of this country, it needs but little to provoke them into actively persecuting those whom they have never ceased to think proper objects of persecution.*

* Ample warning may be drawn from the large infusion of the passions of a persecutor, which mingled with the general display of the worst parts of our national character on the occasion of the Sepoy insurrection. The ravings of fanatics or charlatans from the pulpit may be unworthy of notice; but the heads of the Evangelical party have announced as their principle for the government of Hindus and Mohammedans that no schools be supported by public money in which the Bible is not taught, and by necessary consequence that no public employment be given to any but real or pretended Christians. An Under-Secretary of State, in a speech delivered to his constituents on the 12th of November, 1857, is reported to have said: 'Toleration of their faith' (the faith of a hundred millions of British subjects), 'the superstition which they called religion, by the

For it is this – it is the opinions men entertain, and the feelings they cherish, respecting those who disown the beliefs they deem important which makes this country not a place of mental freedom. For a long time past, the chief mischief of the legal penalties is that they strengthen the social stigma. It is that stigma which is really effective, and so effective is it that the profession of opinions which are under the ban of society is much less common in England than is, in many other countries, the avowal of those which incur risk of judicial punishment. In respect to all persons but those whose pecuniary circumstances make them independent of the good will of other people, opinion, on this subject, is as efficacious as law; men might as well be imprisoned as excluded from the means of earning their bread. Those whose bread is already secured, and who desire no favours from men in power, or from bodies of men, or from the public, have nothing to fear from the open avowal of any opinions but to be ill-thought of and ill-spoken of, and this it ought not to require a very heroic mould to enable them to bear. There is no room for any appeal *ad misericordiam*[13] in behalf of such persons. But though we do not now inflict so much evil on those who think differently from us as it was formerly our custom to do, it may be that we do ourselves as much evil as ever by our treatment of them. Socrates was put to death, but the Socratic philosophy rose like the sun in

---

British Government, had had the effect of retarding the ascendancy of the British name, and preventing the salutary growth of Christianity ... Toleration was the great cornerstone of the religious liberties of this country; but do not let them abuse that precious word "toleration". As he understood it, it meant the complete liberty to all, freedom of worship, *among Christians, who worshiped upon the same foundation.* It meant toleration of all sects and denominations of *Christians who believed in the one mediation.'* I desire to call attention to the fact that a man who has been deemed fit to fill a high office in the government of this country under a liberal ministry maintains the doctrine that all who do not believe in the divinity of Christ are beyond the pale of toleration. Who, after this imbecile display, can indulge the illusion that religious persecution has passed away, never to return?

13. Appeal to compassion.

heaven and spread its illumination over the whole intellectual firmament. Christians were cast to the lions, but the Christian church grew up a stately and spreading tree, overtopping the older and less vigorous growths, and stifling them by its shade. Our merely social intolerance kills no one, roots out no opinions, but induces men to disguise them or to abstain from any active effort for their diffusion. With us, heretical opinions do not perceptibly gain, or even lose, ground in each decade or generation; they never blaze out far and wide, but continue to smoulder in the narrow circles of thinking and studious persons among whom they originate, without ever lighting up the general affairs of mankind with either a true or a deceptive light. And thus is kept up a state of things very satisfactory to some minds, because, without the unpleasant process of fining or imprisoning anybody, it maintains all prevailing opinions outwardly undisturbed, while it does not absolutely interdict the exercise of reason by dissentients afflicted with the malady of thought. A convenient plan for having peace in the intellectual world, and keeping all things going on therein very much as they do already. But the price paid for this sort of intellectual pacification is the sacrifice of the entire moral courage of the human mind. A state of things in which a large portion of the most active and inquiring intellects find it advisable to keep the general principles and grounds of their convictions within their own breasts, and attempt, in what they address to the public, to fit as much as they can of their own conclusions to premises which they have internally renounced, cannot send forth the open, fearless characters and logical, consistent intellects who once adorned the thinking world. The sort of men who can be looked for under it are either mere conformers to commonplace, or timeservers for truth, whose arguments on all great subjects are meant for their hearers, and are not those which have convinced themselves. Those who avoid this alternative do so by narrowing their thoughts and interest to things which can be spoken of without venturing within the region of principles, that is, to small practical matters which would come right of themselves, if but the minds of mankind were strengthened and enlarged, and which will never be made effectually right until then, while that which would strengthen and enlarge men's minds – free and daring speculation on the highest subjects – is abandoned.

Those in whose eyes this reticence on the part of heretics is no evil should consider, in the first place, that in consequence of it there is never any fair and thorough discussion of heretical opinions; and that such of them as could not stand such a discussion, though they may be prevented from spreading, do not disappear. But it is not the minds of heretics that are deteriorated most by the ban placed on all inquiry which does not end in the orthodox conclusions. The greatest harm done is to those who are not heretics, and whose whole mental development is cramped and their reason cowed by the fear of heresy. Who can compute what the world loses in the multitude of promising intellects combined with timid characters, who dare not follow out any bold, vigorous, independent train of thought, lest it should land them in something which would admit of being considered irreligious or immoral? Among them we may occasionally see some man of deep conscientiousness and subtle and refined understanding, who spends a life in sophisticating with an intellect which he cannot silence, and exhausts the resources of ingenuity in attempting to reconcile the promptings of his conscience and reason with orthodoxy, which yet he does not, perhaps, to the end succeed in doing. No one can be a great thinker who does not recognize that as a thinker it is his first duty to follow his intellect to whatever conclusions it may lead. Truth gains more even by the errors of one who, with due study and preparation, thinks for himself than by the true opinions of those who only hold them because they do not suffer themselves to think. Not that it is solely, or chiefly, to form great thinkers that freedom of thinking is required. On the contrary, it is as much and even more indispensable to enable average human beings to attain the mental stature which they are capable of. There have been, and may again be, great individual thinkers in a general atmosphere of mental slavery. But there never has been, nor ever will be, in that atmosphere an intellectually active people.

Where any people has made a temporary approach to such a character, it has been because the dread of heterodox speculation was for a time suspended. Where there is a tacit convention that principles are not to be disputed, where the discussion of the greatest questions which can occupy humanity is considered to be closed, we cannot hope to find that generally high scale of mental activity which has made some periods of history so remarkable. Never when controversy avoided the subjects which are large and important enough to kindle enthusiasm was the mind of a people stirred up from its foundations, and the impulse given which raised even persons of the most ordinary intellect to something of the dignity of thinking beings. Of such we have had an example in the condition of Europe during the times immediately following the Reformation; another, though limited to the Continent and to a more cultivated class, in the speculative movement of the latter half of the eighteenth century; and a third, of still briefer duration, in the intellectual fermentation of Germany during the Goethian and Fichtean period.[14] These periods differed widely in the particular opinions which they developed, but were alike in this, that during all three the yoke of authority was broken. In each, an old mental despotism had been thrown off, and no new one had yet taken its place. The impulse given at these three periods has made Europe what it now is. Every single improvement which has taken place either in the human mind or in institutions may be traced distinctly to one or other of them. Appearances have for some time indicated that all three impulses are well-nigh spent; and we can expect no fresh start until we again assert our mental freedom.

Let us now pass to the second division of the argument, and dismissing the supposition that any of the received opinions may be false, let us assume them to be true and examine into the worth of the manner in which they are likely to be held when their truth is not freely and openly canvassed. However

14. 'Goethian and Fichtean period' is a rather awkward way of designating the romanticism and philosophical idealism of the late 18th and early 19th centuries.

unwillingly a person who has a strong opinion may admit the possibility that his opinion may be false, he ought to be moved by the consideration that, however true it may be, if it is not fully, frequently, and fearlessly discussed, it will be held as a dead dogma, not a living truth.

There is a class of persons (happily not quite so numerous as formerly) who think it enough if a person assents undoubtingly to what they think true, though he has no knowledge whatever of the grounds of the opinion and could not make a tenable defence of it against the most superficial objections. Such persons, if they can once get their creed taught from authority, naturally think that no good, and some harm, comes of its being allowed to be questioned. Where their influence prevails, they make it nearly impossible for the received opinion to be rejected wisely and considerately, though it may still be rejected rashly and ignorantly; for to shut out discussion entirely is seldom possible, and when it once gets in, beliefs not grounded on conviction are apt to give way before the slightest semblance of an argument. Waiving, however, this possibility – assuming that the true opinion abides in the mind, but abides as a prejudice, a belief independent of, and proof against, argument – this is not the way in which truth ought to be held by a rational being. This is not knowing the truth. Truth, thus held, is but one superstition the more, accidentally clinging to the words which enunciate a truth.

If the intellect and judgement of mankind ought to be cultivated, a thing which Protestants at least do not deny, on what can these faculties be more appropriately exercised by anyone than on the things which concern him so much that it is considered necessary for him to hold opinions on them? If the cultivation of the understanding consists in one thing more than in another, it is surely in learning the grounds of one's own opinions. Whatever people believe, on subjects on which it is of the first importance to believe rightly, they ought to be able to defend against at least the common objections. But, someone may say, 'Let them be *taught* the grounds of their opinions. It does not follow that opinions must be merely parroted because they are never heard controverted. Persons who learn geometry do not simply commit the theorems to memory, but understand and learn likewise the demonstrations; and it would be absurd to say that they remain ignorant of the grounds of geometrical truths because they never hear anyone deny and attempt to disprove them.' Undoubtedly: and such teaching suffices on a subject like mathematics, where there is nothing at all to be said on the wrong side of the question. The peculiarity of the evidence of mathematical truths is that all the argument is on one side. There are no objections, and no answers to objections. But on every subject on which difference of opinion is possible, the truth depends on a balance to be struck between two sets of conflicting reasons. Even in natural philosophy, there is always some other explanation possible of the same facts; some geocentric theory instead of heliocentric, some phlogiston instead of oxygen; and it has to be shown why that other theory cannot be the true one; and until this is shown, and until we know how it is shown, we do not understand the grounds of our opinion. But when we turn to subjects infinitely more complicated, to morals, religion, politics, social relations, and the business of life, three-fourths of the arguments for every disputed opinion consist in dispelling the appearances which favour some opinion different from it. The greatest orator, save one, of antiquity, has left it on record that he always studied his adversary's case with as great, if not still greater, intensity than even his own. What Cicero practised as the means of forensic success requires to be imitated by all who study any subject in order to arrive at the truth. He who knows only his own side of the case knows little of that. His reasons may be good, and no one may have been able to refute them. But if he is equally unable to refute the reasons on the opposite side, if he does not so much as know what they are, he has no ground for preferring either opinion. The rational position for him would be suspension of judgement, and unless he contents himself with that, he is either led by authority or adopts, like the generality of the world, the side to which he feels most inclination. Nor is it enough that he should hear the arguments of adversaries from his own teachers, presented as they state them, and accompanied by what they offer as refutations. That is not the way to do justice to the arguments or bring them into real contact with his own mind. He must be able to hear them from persons who actually believe them, who defend them in earnest and do their very utmost for them. He must know them in their most plausible and persuasive form; he must feel the whole force of the difficulty which the true view of the subject has to encounter and dispose of, else he will never really possess himself of the portion of truth which meets and removes that difficulty. Ninety-nine in a hundred of what are called educated men are in this condition, even of those who can argue fluently for their opinions. Their conclusion may be true, but it might be false for anything they know; they have never thrown themselves into the mental position of those who think differently from them, and considered what such persons may have to say; and, consequently, they do not, in any proper sense of the word, know the doctrine which they themselves profess. They do not know those parts of it which explain and justify the remainder – the considerations which show that a fact which seemingly conflicts with another is reconcilable with it, or that, of two apparently strong reasons, one and not the other ought to be preferred. All that part of the truth which turns the scale and decides the judgement of a completely informed mind, they are strangers to; nor is it ever really known but to those who have attended equally and impartially to both sides and endeavoured to see the reasons of both in the strongest light. So essential is this discipline to a real understanding of moral and human subjects that, if opponents of all-important truths do not exist, it is indispensable to imagine them and supply them with the strongest arguments which the most skilful devil's advocate can conjure up.

To abate the force of these considerations, an enemy of free discussion may be supposed to say that there is no necessity for mankind in general to know and understand all that can be said against or for their opinions by philosophers and theologians. That it is not needful for common men to be able to expose all the mis-statements or fallacies of an ingenious opponent. That it is enough if there is always somebody capable of answering them, so that nothing likely to mislead uninstructed persons remains unrefuted. That simple minds, having been taught the obvious grounds of the truths inculcated in them, may trust to authority for the rest and, being aware that they have neither knowledge nor talent to resolve every difficulty which can be raised, may repose in the assurance that all those which have been raised have been or can be answered by those who are specially trained to the task.

Conceding to this view of the subject the utmost that can be claimed for it by those most easily satisfied with the amount of understanding of truth which ought to accompany the belief of it, even so, the argument for free discussion is noway weakened. For even this doctrine acknowledges that mankind ought to have a rational assurance that all objections have been satisfactorily answered; and how are they to be answered if that which requires to be answered is not spoken? Or how can the answer be known to be satisfactory if the objectors have no opportunity of showing that it is unsatisfactory? If not the public, at least the philosophers and theologians who are to resolve the difficulties must make themselves familiar with those difficulties in their most puzzling form; and this cannot be accomplished unless they are freely stated and placed in the most advantageous light which they admit of. The Catholic Church has its own way of dealing with this embarrassing problem. It makes a broad separation between those who can be permitted to receive its doctrines on conviction and those who must accept them on trust. Neither, indeed, are allowed any choice as to what they will accept; but the clergy, such at least as can be fully confided in, may admissibly and meritoriously make themselves acquainted with the arguments of opponents, in order to answer them, and may, therefore, read heretical books; the laity, not unless by special permission, hard to be obtained. This discipline recognizes a knowledge of the enemy's case as beneficial to the teachers, but finds means, consistent with this, of denying it to the rest of the world, thus giving to the *élite* more mental culture, though not more mental freedom, than it allows to the mass. By this device it succeeds in obtaining the kind of mental superiority which its purposes require: for though culture without freedom never made a large and liberal mind, it can make a clever *nisi prius*[15] advocate of a cause. But in countries professing Protestantism, this resource is denied, since Protestants hold, at least in theory, that the responsibility for the choice of a religion must be borne by each for himself and cannot be thrown off upon teachers. Besides, in the present state of the world, it is practically impossible that writings which are read by the instructed can be kept from the uninstructed. If the teachers of mankind are to be cognizant of all that they ought to know, everything must be free to be written and published without restraint.

If, however, the mischievous operation of the absence of free discussion, when the received opinions are true, were confined to leaving men ignorant of the grounds of those opinions, it might be thought that this, if an intellectual, is no moral evil and does not affect the worth of the opinions, regarded in their influence on the character. The fact, however, is that not only the grounds of the opinion are forgotten in the absence of discussion, but too often the meaning of the opinion itself. The words which convey it cease to suggest ideas, or suggest only a small portion of those they were originally employed to communicate. Instead of a vivid conception and a living belief, there remain only a few phrases retained by rote; or, if any part, the shell and husk only of the meaning is retained, the finer essence being lost. The great chapter in human history which this fact occupies and fills cannot be too earnestly studied and meditated on.

It is illustrated in the experience of almost all ethical doctrines and religious creeds. They are all full of meaning and vitality to those who originate them, and to the direct disciples of the originators. Their meaning continues to be felt in undiminished strength, and is perhaps brought out into even fuller consciousness, so long as the struggle lasts to give the doctrine or creed an ascendancy over other creeds. At last it either prevails and becomes the general opinion, or its progress stops; it keeps possession of the ground it has

15. A civil action, a trial before judge and jury.

gained, but ceases to spread further. When either of these results has become apparent, controversy on the subject flags, and gradually dies away. The doctrine has taken its place, if not as a received opinion, as one of the admitted sects or divisions of opinion; those who hold it have generally inherited, not adopted it; and conversion from one of these doctrines to another, being now an exceptional fact, occupies little place in the thoughts of their professors. Instead of being, as at first, constantly on the alert either to defend themselves against the world or to bring the world over to them, they have subsided into acquiescence and neither listen, when they can help it, to arguments against their creed, nor trouble dissentients (if there be such) with arguments in its favour. From this time may usually be dated the decline in the living power of the doctrine. We often hear the teachers of all creeds lamenting the difficulty of keeping up in the minds of believers a lively apprehension of the truth which they nominally recognize, so that it may penetrate the feelings and acquire a real mastery over the conduct. No such difficulty is complained of while the creed is still fighting for its existence; even the weaker combatants then know and feel what they are fighting for, and the difference between it and other doctrines; and in that period of every creed's existence not a few persons may be found who have realized its fundamental principles in all the forms of thought, have weighed and considered them in all their important bearings, and have experienced the full effect on the character which belief in that creed ought to produce in a mind thoroughly inbued with it. But when it has come to be an hereditary creed, and to be received passively, not actively – when the mind is no longer compelled, in the same degree as at first, to exercise its vital powers on the questions which its belief presents to it, there is a progressive tendency to forget all of the belief except the formularies, or to give it a dull and torpid assent, as if accepting it on trust dispensed with the necessity of realizing it in consciousness, or testing it by personal experience, until it almost ceases to connect itself at all with the inner life of the human being. Then are seen the cases, so frequent in this age of the world as almost to form the majority, in which the creed remains as it were outside the mind, incrusting and petrifying it against all other influences addressed to the higher parts of our nature; manifesting its power by not suffering any fresh and living conviction to get in, but itself doing nothing for the mind or heart except standing sentinel over them to keep them vacant.

To what an extent doctrines intrinsically fitted to make the deepest impression upon the mind may remain in it as dead beliefs, without being ever realized in the imagination, the feelings, or the understanding, is exemplified by the manner in which the majority of believers hold the doctrines of Christianity. By Christianity, I here mean what is accounted such by all churches and sects – the maxims and precepts contained in the New Testament. These are considered sacred, and accepted as laws, by all professing Christians. Yet it is scarcely too much to say that not one Christian in a thousand guides or tests his individual conduct by reference to those laws. The standard to which he does refer it is the custom of his nation, his class, or his religious profession. He has thus, on the one hand, a collection of ethical maxims which he believes to have been vouchsafed to him by infallible wisdom as rules for his government; and, on the other, a set of everyday judgements and practices which go a certain length with some of those maxims, not so great a length with others, stand in direct opposition to some, and are, on the whole, a compromise between the Christian creed and the interests and suggestions of worldly life. To the first of these standards he gives his homage; to the other his real allegiance. All Christians believe that the blessed are the poor and humble, and those who are ill-used by the world; that it is easier for a camel to pass through the eye of a needle than for a rich man to enter the kingdom of heaven; that they should judge not, lest they be judged; that they should swear not at all; that they should love their neighbour as themselves; that if one take their cloak, they should give him their coat also; that they should take no thought for the morrow; that if they would be perfect they should sell all that they have and give it to the poor. They are not insincere when they say that they believe these things.

They do believe them, as people believe what they have always heard lauded and never discussed. But in the sense of that living belief which regulates conduct, they believe these doctrines just up to the point to which it is usual to act upon them. The doctrines in their integrity are serviceable to pelt adversaries with; and it is understood that they are to be put forward (when possible) as the reasons for whatever people do that they think laudable. But anyone who reminded them that the maxims require an infinity of things which they never even think of doing would gain nothing but to be classed among those very unpopular characters who affect to be better than other people. The doctrines have no hold on ordinary believers – are not a power in their minds. They have an habitual respect for the sound of them, but no feeling which spreads from the words to the things signified and forces the mind to take *them* in and make them conform to the formula. Whenever conduct is concerned, they look round for Mr A and B to direct them how far to go in obeying Christ.

Now we may be well assured that the case was not thus, but far otherwise, with the early Christians. Had it been thus, Christianity never would have expanded from an obscure sect of the despised Hebrews into the religion of the Roman empire. When their enemies said, 'See how these Christians love one another' (a remark not likely to be made by anybody now), they assuredly had a much livelier feeling of the meaning of their creed than they have ever had since. And to this cause, probably, it is chiefly owing that Christianity now makes so little progress in extending its domain, and after eighteen centuries is still nearly confined to Europeans and the descendants of Europeans. Even with the strictly religious, who are much in earnest about their doctrines and attach a greater amount of meaning to many of them than people in general, it commonly happens that the part which is thus comparatively active in their minds is that which was made by Calvin, or Knox,[16] or some such person much nearer in character to themselves. The sayings of Christ coexist passively in their

16. For Mills' views of John Calvin (and of his Scottish disciple, John Knox), see *On Liberty* below, pp. 126-7.

minds, producing hardly any effect beyond what is caused by mere listening to words so amiable and bland. There are many reasons, doubtless, why doctrines which are the badge of a sect retain more of their vitality than those common to all recognized sects, and why more pains are taken by teachers to keep their meaning alive; but one reason certainly is that the peculiar doctrines are more questioned and have to be oftener defended against open gainsayers. Both teachers and learners go to sleep at their post as soon as there is no enemy in the field.

The same thing holds true, generally speaking, of all traditional doctrines – those of prudence and knowledge of life as well as of morals or religion. All languages and literatures are full of general observations on life, both as to what it is and how to conduct oneself in it – observations which everybody knows, which everybody repeats or hears with acquiescence, which are received as truisms, yet of which most people first truly learn the meaning when experience, generally of a painful kind, has made it a reality to them. How often, when smarting under some unforeseen misfortune or disappointment, does a person call to mind some proverb or common saying, familiar to him all his life, the meaning of which, if he had ever before felt it as he does now, would have saved him from the calamity. There are indeed reasons for this, other than the absence of discussion; there are many truths of which the full meaning *cannot* be realized until personal experience has brought it home. But much more of the meaning even of these would have been understood, and what was understood would have been far more deeply impressed on the mind, if the man had been accustomed to hear it argued *pro* and *con* by people who did understand it. The fatal tendency of mankind to leave off thinking about a thing when it is no longer doubtful is the cause of half their errors. A contemporary author has well spoken of 'the deep slumber of a decided opinion'.

But what! (it may be asked), Is the absence of unanimity an indispensable condition of true knowledge? Is it necessary that some part of mankind should persist in error to enable any to realize the truth? Does a belief cease to be real and vital as soon as it is generally received – and is a proposition never thoroughly understood and felt unless some doubt of it remains? As soon as mankind have unanimously accepted a truth, does the truth perish within them? The highest aim and best result of improved intelligence, it has hitherto been thought, is to unite mankind more and more in the acknowledgement of all-important truths; and does the intelligence only last as long as it has not achieved its object? Do the fruits of conquest perish by the very completeness of the victory?

I affirm no such thing. As mankind improve, the number of doctrines which are no longer disputed or doubted will be constantly on the increase; and the well-being of mankind may almost be measured by the number and gravity of the truths which have reached the point of being uncontested. The cessation, on one question after another, of serious controversy is one of the necessary incidents of the consolidation of opinion – a consolidation as salutary in the case of true opinions as it is dangerous and noxious when the opinions are erroneous. But though this gradual narrowing of the bounds of diversity of opinion is necessary in both senses of the term, being at once inevitable and indispensable, we are not therefore obliged to conclude that all its consequences must be beneficial. The loss of so important an aid to the intelligent and living apprehension of a truth as is afforded by the necessity of explaining it to, or defending it against, opponents, though not sufficient to outweigh, is no trifling drawback from the benefit of its universal recognition. Where this advantage can no longer be had, I confess I should like to see the teachers of mankind endeavouring to provide a substitute for it – some contrivance for making the difficulties of the question as present to the learner's consciousness as if they were pressed upon him by a dissentient champion, eager for his conversion.

But instead of seeking contrivances for this purpose, they have lost those they formerly had. The Socratic dialectics, so magnificently exemplified in the dialogues of Plato, were a contrivance of this description. They were essentially a negative discussion of the great questions of philosophy and life, directed with consummate skill to the purpose of convincing anyone who had merely adopted the commonplaces of received opinion that he did not understand the subject – that he as yet attached no definite meaning to the doctrines he professed; in order that, becoming aware of his ignorance, he might be put in the way to obtain a stable belief, resting on a clear apprehension both of the meaning of doctrines and of their evidence. The school disputations of the Middle Ages had a somewhat similar object. They were intended to make sure that the pupil understood his own opinion, and (by necessary correlation) the opinion opposed to it, and could enforce the grounds of the one and confute those of the other. These last-mentioned contests had indeed the incurable defect that the premises appealed to were taken from authority, not from reason; and, as a discipline to the mind, they were in every respect inferior to the powerful dialectics which formed the intellects of the *Socratici viri*,[17] but the modern mind owes far more to both than it is generally willing to admit, and the present modes of education contain nothing which in the smallest degree supplies the place either of the one or of the other. A person who derives all his instruction from teachers or books, even if he escape the besetting temptation of contenting himself with cram, is under no compulsion to hear both sides; accordingly it is far from a frequent accomplishment, even among thinkers, to know both sides; and the weakest part of what everybody says in defence of his opinion is what he intends as a reply to antagonists. It is the fashion of the present time to disparage negative logic – that which points out weaknesses in theory or errors in practice without establishing positive truths. Such negative criticism would indeed be poor enough as an ultimate result, but as a means to attaining any positive knowledge or conviction worthy the name it cannot be valued too highly; and until people are again systematically trained to it, there will be few great thinkers and a low general average of intellect in any but the mathematical and physical departments of speculation. On any other subject no one's opinions deserve the name of knowledge,

17. The Socratic men – i.e., the disciples of Socrates.

except so far as he has either had forced upon him by others or gone through of himself the same mental process which would have been required of him in carrying on an active controversy with opponents. That, therefore, which, when absent, it is so indispensable, but so difficult, to create, how worse than absurd it is to forego when spontaneously offering itself! If there are any persons who contest a received opinion, or who will do so if law or opinion will let them, let us thank them for it, open our minds to listen to them, and rejoice that there is someone to do for us what we otherwise ought, if we have any regard for either the certainty or the vitality of our convictions, to do with much greater labour for ourselves.

It still remains to speak of one of the principal causes which make diversity of opinion advantageous, and will continue to do so until mankind shall have entered a stage of intellectual advancement which at present seems at an incalculable distance. We have hitherto considered only two possibilities: that the received opinion may be false, and some other opinion, consequently, true; or that, the received opinion being true, a conflict with the opposite error is essential to a clear apprehension and deep feeling of its truth. But there is a commoner case than either of these: when the conflicting doctrines, instead of being one true and the other false, share the truth between them, and the nonconforming opinion is needed to supply the remainder of the truth of which the received doctrine embodies only a part. Popular opinions, on subjects not palpable to sense, are often true, but seldom or never the whole truth. They are a part of the truth, sometimes a greater, sometimes a smaller part, but exaggerated, distorted, and disjointed from the truths by which they ought to be accompanied and limited. Heretical opinions, on the other hand, are generally some of these suppressed and neglected truths, bursting the bonds which kept them down, and either seeking reconciliation with the truth contained in the common opinion, or fronting it as enemies, and setting themselves up, with similar exclusiveness, as the whole truth. The latter case is hitherto the most frequent, as, in the human mind, one-sidedness has always been the rule, and many-sidedness the exception. Hence, even in revolutions of opinion, one part of the truth usually sets while another rises. Even progress, which ought to superadd, for the most part only substitutes one partial and incomplete truth for another; improvement consisting chiefly in this, that the new fragment of truth is more wanted, more adapted to the needs of the time than that which it displaces. Such being the partial character of prevailing opinions, even when resting on a true foundation, every opinion which embodies somewhat of the portion of truth which the common opinion omits ought to be considered precious, with whatever amount of error and confusion that truth may be blended. No sober judge of human affairs will feel bound to be indignant because those who force on our notice truths which we should otherwise have overlooked, overlook some of those which we see. Rather, he will think that so long as popular truth is one-sided, it is more desirable than otherwise that unpopular truth should have one-sided assertors, too, such being usually the most energetic and the most likely to compel reluctant attention to the fragment of wisdom which they proclaim as if it were the whole.

Thus, in the eighteenth century, when nearly all the instructed, and all those of the uninstructed who were led by them, were lost in admiration of what is called civilization, and of the marvels of modern science, literature, and philosophy, and while greatly overrating the amount of unlikeness between the men of modern and those of ancient times, indulged the belief that the whole of the difference was in their own favour; with what a salutary shock did the paradoxes of Rousseau explode like bombshells in the midst, dislocating the the compact mass of one-sided opinion and forcing its elements to recombine in a better form and with additional ingredients. Not that the current opinions were on the whole farther from the truth than Rousseau's were; on the contrary, they were nearer to it; they contained more of positive truth, and very much less of error. Nevertheless there lay in Rousseau's doctrine, and has floated down the stream of opinion along with it, a considerable amount of exactly those truths which the popular opinion wanted; and these are the deposit which was left behind them when the flood subsided. The superior worth of simplicity of life, the enervating and demoralizing effect of the trammels and hypocrisies of artificial society are ideas which have never been entirely absent from cultivated minds since Rousseau wrote; and and they will in time produce their due effect, though at present needing to be asserted as much as ever, and to be asserted by deeds; for words, on this subject, have nearly exhausted their power.[18]

In politics, again, it is almost a commonplace that a party of order or stability and a party of progress or reform are both necessary elements of a healthy state of political life, until the one or the other shall have so enlarged its mental grasp as to be a party equally of order and of progress, knowing and distinguishing what is fit to be preserved from what ought to be swept away. Each of these modes of thinking derives its utility from the deficiencies of the other; but it is in a great measure the opposition of the other that keeps each within the limits of reason and sanity. Unless opinions favourable to democracy and to aristocracy, to property and to equality, to cooperation and to competition, to luxury and to abstinence, to sociality and individuality, to liberty and discipline, and all the other standing antagonisms of practical life, are expressed with equal freedom and enforced and defended with equal talent and energy, there is no chance of both elements obtaining their due; one scale is sure to go up, and the other down. Truth, in the great practical concerns of life, is so much a question of the reconciling and combining of opposites that very few have minds sufficiently capacious and impartial to make the adjustment with an approach to correctness, and it has to be made by the rough process of a struggle between

18. One might have expected that in a work on liberty Mill would have cited another of Rousseau's 'paradoxes': the idea that man could be 'forced to be free'; that the individual will was best represented in the 'general will'. But here and elsewhere (in his essay on Coleridge, for example), it was the corrupting effect of civilization, the superiority of natural man, that impressed Mill as the essential 'paradox' of Rousseau.

combatants fighting under hostile banners. On any of the great open questions just enumerated, if either of the two opinions has a better claim than the other, not merely to be tolerated, but to be encouraged and countenanced, it is the one which happens at the particular time and place to be in a minority. That is the opinion which for the time being, repre sents the neglected interests, the side of human well-being which is in danger of obtaining less than its share. I am aware that there is not, in this country, any intolerance of differences of opinion on most of these topics. They are adduced to show, by admitted and multiplied examples, the universality of the fact that only through diversity of opinion is there, in the existing state of human intellect, a chance of fair play to all sides of the truth. When there are persons to be found who form an exception to the apparent unanimity of the world on any subject, even if the world is in the right, it is always probable that dissentients have something worth hearing to say for themselves, and that truth would lose something by their silence.

It may be objected, 'But *some* received principles, especially on the highest and most vital subjects, are more than half-truths. The Christian morality, for instance, is the whole truth on that subject, and if anyone teaches a morality which varies from it, he is wholly in error.' As this is of all cases the most important in practice, none can be fitter to test the general maxim. But before pronouncing what Christian morality is or is not, it would be desirable to decide what is meant by Christian morality. If it means the morality of the New Testament, I wonder that any one who derives his knowledge of this from the book itself can suppose that it was announced, or intended, as a complete doctrine of morals. The Gospel always refers to a pre-existing morality and confines its precepts to the particulars in which that morality was to be corrected or superseded by a wider and higher; expressing itself, moreover, in terms most general, often impossible to be interpreted literally, and possessing rather the impressiveness of poetry or eloquence than the precision of legislation. To extract from it a body of ethical doctrine has never been possible without eking it out from the Old Testament, that is, from a system elaborate indeed, but in many respects barbarous, and intended only for a barbarous people. St Paul, a declared enemy to this Judaical mode of interpreting the doctrine and filling up the scheme of his Master, equally assumes a pre-existing morality, namely that of the Greeks and Romans; and his advice to Christians is in a great measure a system of accommodation to that, even to the extent of giving an apparent sanction to slavery. What is called Christian, but should rather be termed theological, morality was not the work of Christ or the Apostles, but is of much later origin, having been gradually built up by the Catholic Church of the first five centuries, and though not implicitly adopted by moderns and Protestants, has been much less modified by them than might have been expected. For the most part, indeed, they have contented themselves with cutting off the additions which had been made to it in the Middle Ages, each sect supplying the place by fresh additions, adapted to its own character and tendencies. That mankind owe a great debt to this morality, and to its early teachers, I should be the last person to deny, but I do not scruple to say of it that it is, in many important points, incomplete and one-sided, and that, unless ideas and feelings not sanctioned by it had contributed to the formation of European life and character, human affairs would have been in a worse condition than they now are. Christian morality (so called) has all the characters of a reaction; it is, in great part, a protest against paganism. Its ideal is negative rather than positive; passive rather than active; innocence rather than nobleness; abstinence from evil rather than energetic pursuit of good; in its precepts (as has been well said) 'thou shalt not' predominates unduly over 'thou shalt'. In its horror of sensuality, it made an idol of asceticism which has been gradually compromised away into one of legality. It holds out the hope of heaven and the threat of hell as the appointed and appropriate motives to a virtuous life: in this falling far below the best of the ancients, and doing what lies in it to give to human morality an essentially selfish character, by disconnecting each man's feelings of duty from the interests of his fellow creatures, except so far as a self-interested inducement is offered to him for consulting them. It is essentially a doctrine of passive obedience; it inculcates submission to all authorities found established; who indeed are not to be actively obeyed when they command what religion forbids, but who are not to be resisted, far less rebelled against, for any amount of wrong to ourselves. And while, in the morality of the best pagan nations, duty to the State holds even a disproportionate place, infringing on the just liberty of the individual, in purely Christian ethics that grand department of duty is scarcely noticed or acknowledged. It is in the Koran, not the New Testament, that we read the maxim: 'A ruler who appoints any man to an office, when there is in his dominions another man better qualified for it, sins against God and against the State.' What little recognition the idea of obligation to the public obtains in modern morality is derived from Greek and Roman sources, not from Christian; as, even in the morality of private life, whatever exists of magnanimity, high-mindedness, personal dignity, even the sense of honour, is derived from the purely human, not the religious part of our education, and never could have grown out of a standard of ethics in which the only worth, professedly recognized, is that of obedience.

I am as far as anyone from pretending that these defects are necessarily inherent in the Christian ethics in every manner in which it can be conceived, or that the many requisites of a complete moral doctrine which it does not contain do not admit of being reconciled with it. Far less would I insinuate this out of the doctrines and precepts of Christ himself. I believe that the sayings of Christ are all that I can see any evidence of their having been intended to be; that they are irreconcilable with nothing which a comprehensive morality requires; that everything which is excellent in ethics may be brought within them, with no greater violence to their language than has been done to it by all who have attempted to deduce from them any practical system of conduct whatever. But it is quite consistent with this to believe that they contain, and were meant to contain, only a part of the truth; that many essential elements of the highest morality are among the things which are not provided for, nor intended to be provided for, in the recorded deliverances of the Founder of Christianity, and which have been entirely thrown aside in the system of ethics erected on the basis of those deliverances by the Christian Church. And this being so, I think it a great error to persist in attempting to find in the Christian doctrine that complete rule for our guidance which its Author intended it to sanction and enforce, but only partially to provide. I believe, too, that this narrow theory is becoming a grave practical evil, detracting greatly from the moral training and instruction which so many well-meaning persons are now at length exerting themselves to promote. I much fear that by attempting to form the mind and feelings on an exclusively religious type, and discarding those secular standards (as for want of a better name they may be called) which heretofore coexisted with and supplemented the Christian ethics, receiving some of its spirit, and infusing into it some of theirs, there will result, and is even now resulting, a low, abject, servile type of character which, submit itself as it may to what it deems the Supreme Will, is incapable of rising to or sympathizing in the conception of Supreme Goodness. I believe that other ethics than any which can be evolved from exclusively Christian sources must exist side by side with Christian ethics to produce the moral regeneration of mankind; and that the Christian system is no exception to the rule that in an imperfect state of the human mind the interests of truth require a diversity of opinions. It is not necessary that in ceasing to ignore the moral truths not contained in Christianity men should ignore any of those which it does contain. Such prejudice or oversight, when it occurs, is altogether an evil, but it is one from which we cannot hope to be always exempt, and must be regarded as the price paid for an inestimable good. The exclusive pretension made by a part of the truth to be the whole must and ought to be protested against; and if a reactionary impulse should make the protestors unjust in their turn, this one-sidedness, like the other, may be lamented but must be tolerated. If Christians would teach infidels to be just to Christianity, they should themselves be just to infidelity. It can do truth no service to blink the fact, known to all who have the most ordinary acquaintance with literary history, that a large portion of the noblest and most valuable moral teaching has been the work, not only of men who did not know, but of men who knew and rejected, the Christian faith.

I do not pretend that the most unlimited use of the freedom of enunciating all possible opinions would put an end to the evils of religious or philosophical sectarianism. Every truth which men of narrow capacity are in earnest about is sure to be asserted, inculcated, and in many ways even acted on, as if no other truth existed in the world, or at all events none that could limit or qualify the first. I acknowledge that the tendency of all opinions to become sectarian is not cured by the freest discussion, but is often heightened and exacerbated thereby: the truth which ought to have been, but was not, seen, being rejected all the more violently because proclaimed by persons regarded as opponents. But it is not on the impassioned partisan, it is on the calmer and more disinterested bystander, that this collision of opinions works its salutary effect. Not the violent conflict between parts of the truth, but the quiet suppression of half of it, is the formidable evil; there is always hope when people are forced to listen to both sides; it is when they attend only to one that errors harden into prejudices, and truth itself ceases to have the effect of truth by being exaggerated into falsehood. And since there are few mental attributes more rare than that judicial faculty which can sit in intelligent judgement between two sides of a question, of which only one is represented by an advocate before it, truth has no chance but in proportion as every side of it, every opinion which embodies any fraction of the truth, not only finds advocates, but is so advocated as to be listened to.

We have now recognized the necessity to the mental well-being of mankind (on which all their other well-being depends) of freedom of opinion, and freedom of the expression of opinion, on four distinct grounds, which we will now briefly recapitulate:

First, if any opinion is compelled to silence, that opinion

may, for aught we can certainly know, be true. To deny this is to assume our own infallibility.

Secondly, though the silenced opinion be an error, it may, and very commonly does, contain a portion of truth; and since the general or prevailing opinion on any subject is rarely or never the whole truth, it is only by the collision of adverse opinions that the remainder of the truth has any chance of being supplied.

Thirdly, even if the received opinion be not only true, but the whole truth; unless it is suffered to be, and actually is, vigorously and earnestly contested, it will, by most of those who receive it, be held in the manner of a prejudice, with little comprehension or feeling of its rational grounds. And not only this, but, fourthly, the meaning of the doctrine itself will be in danger of being lost or enfeebled, and deprived of its vital effect on the character and conduct: the dogma becoming a mere formal profession, inefficacious for good, but cumbering the ground and preventing the growth of any real and heartfelt conviction from reason or personal experience.

Before quitting the subject of freedom of opinion, it is fit to take some notice of those who say that the free expression of all opinions should be permitted on condition that the manner be temperate, and do not pass the bounds of fair discussion. Much might be said on the impossibility of fixing where these supposed bounds are to be placed; for if the test be offence to those whose opinions are attacked, I think experience testifies that this offence is given whenever the attack is telling and powerful, and that every opponent who pushes them hard, and whom they find it difficult to answer, appears to them, if he shows any strong feeling on the subject, an intemperate opponent. But this, though an important consideration in a practical point of view, merges in a more fundamental objection. Undoubtedly, the manner of asserting an opinion, even though it be a true one, may be very objectionable and may justly incur severe censure. But the principal offences of the kind are such as it is mostly impossible, unless by accidental self-betrayal, to bring home to conviction. The gravest of them is, to argue sophistically, to suppress facts or arguments, to misstate the elements of the case, or misrepresent the opposite opinion. But all this, even to the most aggravated degree, is so continually done in perfect good faith by persons who are not considered, and in many other respects may not deserve to be considered, ignorant or incompetent, that it is rarely possible, on adequate grounds, conscientiously to stamp the misrepresentation as morally culpable, and still less could law presume to interfere with this kind of controversial misconduct. With regard to what is commonly meant by intemperate discussion, namely invective, sarcasm, personality, and the like, the denunciation of these weapons would deserve more sympathy if it were ever proposed to interdict them equally to both sides; but it is only desired to restrain the employment of them against the prevailing opinion; against the unprevailing they may not only be used without general disapproval, but will be likely to obtain for him who uses them the praise of honest zeal and righteous indignation. Yet whatever mischief arises from their use is greatest when they are employed against the comparatively defenceless; and whatever unfair advantage can be derived by any opinion from this mode of asserting it accrues almost exclusively to received opinions. The worst offence of this kind which can be committed by a polemic is to stigmatize those who hold the contrary opinion as bad and immoral men. To calumny of this sort, those who hold any unpopular opinion are peculiarly exposed, because they are in general few and uninfluential, and nobody but themselves feels much interested in seeing justice done them; but this weapon is, from the nature of the case, denied to those who attack a prevailing opinion: they can neither use it with safety to themselves, nor, if they could, would it do anything but recoil on their own cause. In general, opinions contrary to those commonly received can only obtain a hearing by studied moderation of language and the most cautious avoidance of unnecessary offence, from which they hardly ever deviate even in a slight degree without losing ground, while unmeasured vituperation employed on the side of the prevailing opinion really does deter people from professing contrary opinions and from listening to those who profess them. For the interest, therefore, of truth and justice it is far more important to restrain this employment of vituperative language than the other; and, for example if it were necessary to choose, there would be much more need to discourage offensive attacks on infidelity than on religion. It is, however, obvious that law and authority have no business with restraining either, while opinion ought, in every instance, to determine its verdict by the circumstances of the individual case – condemning everyone, on whichever side of the argument he places himself, in whose mode of advocacy either want of candour, or malignity, bigotry, or intolerance of feeling manifest themselves; but not inferring these vices from the side which a person takes, though it be the contrary side of the question to our own; and giving merited honour to everyone, whatever opinion he may hold, who has calmness to see and honesty to state what his opponents and their opinions really are, exaggerating nothing to their discredit, keeping nothing back which tells, or can be supposed to tell, in their favour. This is the real morality of public discussion; and if often violated, I am happy to think that there are many controversialists who to a great extent observe it, and a still greater number who conscientiously strive towards it.

CHAPTER III

Of Individuality,
as One of the
Elements of Well-Being

SUCH being the reasons which make it imperative that human beings should be free to form opinions and to express their opinions without reserve; and such the baneful consequences to the intellectual, and through that to the moral nature of man, unless this liberty is either conceded or asserted in spite of prohibition; let us next examine whether the same reasons do not require that men should be free to act upon their opinions – to carry these out in their lives without hindrance, either physical or moral, from their fellow men, so long as it is at their own risk and peril. This last proviso is of course indispensable. No one pretends that actions should be as free as opinions. On the contrary, even opinions lose their immunity when the circumstances in which they are expressed are such as to constitute their expression a positive instigation to some mischievous act. An opinion that corn dealers are starvers of the poor, or that private property is robbery, ought to be unmolested when simply circulated through the press, but may justly incur punishment when delivered orally to an excited mob assembled before the house of a corn dealer, or when handed about among the same mob in the form of a placard. Acts, of whatever kind, which without justifiable cause do harm to others may be, and in the more important cases absolutely require to be, controlled by the unfavourable sentiments, and, when needful, by the active interference of mankind. The liberty of the individual must be thus far limited; he must not make himself a nuisance to other people. But if he refrains from molesting others in what concerns them, and merely acts according to his own inclination and judgement in things which concern himself, the same reasons which show that opinion should be free prove also that he should be allowed, without molestation, to carry his opinions into practice at his own cost. That mankind are not infallible; that their truths, for the most part, are only half-truths; that unity of opinion, unless resulting from the fullest and freest comparison of opposite opinions, is not desirable, and diversity not an evil, but a good, until mankind are much more capable than at present of recognizing all sides of the truth, are principles applicable to men's modes of action not less than to their opinions. As it is useful that while mankind are imperfect there should be different opinions, so it is that there should be different experiments of living; that free scope should be given to varieties of character, short of injury to others; and that the worth of different modes of life should be proved practically, when anyone thinks fit to try them. It is desirable, in short, that in things which do not primarily concern others, individuality should assert itself. Where not the person's own character but the traditions or customs of other people are the rule of conduct, there is wanting one of the principal ingredients of human happiness, and quite the chief ingredient of individual and social progress.

In maintaining this principle, the greatest difficulty to be encountered does not lie in the appreciation of means towards an acknowledged end, but in the indifference of persons in general to the end itself. If it were felt that the free development of individuality is one of the leading essentials of well-being; that it is not only a co-ordinate element with all that is designated by the terms civilization, instruction, education, culture, but is itself a necessary part and condition of all those things, there would be no danger that liberty should be undervalued, and the adjustment of the boundaries between it and social control would present no extraordinary difficulty. But the evil is that individual spontaneity is hardly recognized by the common modes of thinking as having any intrinsic worth, or deserving any regard on its own account. The majority, being satisfied with the ways of mankind as they now are (for it is they who make them what they are), cannot comprehend why those ways should not be good enough for everybody; and what is more, spontaneity forms no part of the ideal of the majority of moral and social reformers, but is rather looked on with jealousy, as a troublesome and perhaps rebellious obstruction to the general acceptance of what these reformers, in their own judgement, think would be best for mankind. Few persons, out of Germany, even comprehend the meaning of the doctrine which Wilhelm von Humboldt, so eminent both as a *savant* and as a politician, made the text of a treatise – that 'the end of man, or that which is prescribed by the eternal or immutable dictates of reason, and not suggested by vague and transient desires, is the highest and most harmonious development of his powers to a complete and consistent whole'; that, therefore, the object 'towards which every human being must ceaselessly direct his efforts, and on which especially those who design to influence their fellow men must ever keep their eyes, is the individuality of power and development'; that for this there are two requisites, 'freedom, and variety of situations'; and that from the union of these arise 'individual vigour and manifold diversity', which combine themselves in 'originality'.*

Little, however, as people are accustomed to a doctrine like that of von Humboldt, and surprising as it may be to them to find so high a value attached to individuality, the question, one must nevertheless think, can only be one of degree. No

* *The Sphere and Duties of Government*, from the German of Baron Wilhelm von Humboldt, pp. 11–13. [The German title was *Ideen zu einem Versuch die Grenzen der Wirksamkeit des Staats zu bestimmen*. It has recently been re-issued in English under the title *The Limits of State Action*, edited by J. W. Burrow, Cambridge, 1969. Written by Humboldt (1767–1835), in 1791–2, only short sections of it were released at the time, the book as a whole being published in Germany posthumously, in 1852, as part of a complete edition of his works. The English translation appeared in 1854, when Mill had just started to write *On Liberty*. It is ironic that Humboldt's fame in his own time came not from this exceedingly laissez-fairist book but from his position as Minister of Public Instruction; he founded the University of Berlin, reorganized the Prussian *Gymnasium* (the secondary school), and tried to impress upon both, his conception of culture. It is ironic too that Matthew Arnold should also have been a great admirer of Humboldt, but for different reasons from Mill's. One of Humboldt's educational memoranda appeared as the epigraph to Arnold's *Schools and Universities on the Continent* (1868): 'The thing is *not* to let the schools and universities go on in a drowsy and impotent routine; the thing is, to raise the culture of the nation ever higher and higher by their means.']

one's idea of excellence in conduct is that people should do absolutely nothing but copy one another. No one would assert that people ought not to put into their mode of life, and into the conduct of their concerns, any impress whatever of their own judgement or of their own individual character. On the other hand, it would be absurd to pretend that people ought to live as if nothing whatever had been known in the world before they came into it; as if experience had as yet done nothing towards showing that one mode of existence, or of conduct, is preferable to another. Nobody denies that people should be so taught and trained in youth as to know and benefit by the ascertained results of human experience. But it is the privilege and proper condition of a human being, arrived at the maturity of his faculties, to use and interpret experience in his own way. It is for him to find out what part of recorded experience is properly applicable to his own circumstances and character. The traditions and customs of other people are, to a certain extent, evidence of what their experience has taught *them* – presumptive evidence, and as such, have a claim to his deference: but, in the first place, their experience may be too narrow, or they may have not interpreted it rightly. Secondly, their interpretation of experience may be correct, but unsuitable to him. Customs are made for customary circumstances and customary characters; and his circumstances or his character may be uncustomary. Thirdly, though the customs be both good as customs and suitable to him, yet to conform to custom merely *as* custom does not educate or develop in him any of the qualities which are the distinctive endowment of a human being. The human faculties of perception, judgement, discriminative feeling, mental activity, and even moral preference are exercised only in making a choice. He who does anything because it is the custom makes no choice. He gains no practice either in discerning or in desiring what is best. The mental and moral, like the muscular, powers are improved only by being used. The faculties are called into no exercise by doing a thing merely because others do it, no more than by believing a thing only because others believe it. If the grounds of an opinion are not conclusive to the person's own reason, his reason cannot be strengthened, but is likely to be weakened, by his adopting it: and if the inducements to an act are not such as are consentaneous to his own feelings and character (where affection, or the rights of others, are not concerned), it is so much done towards rendering his feelings and character inert and torpid instead of active and energetic.

He who lets the world, or his own portion of it, choose his plan of life for him has no need of any other faculty than the ape-like one of imitation. He who chooses his plan for himself employs all his faculties. He must use observation to see, reasoning and judgement to foresee, activity to gather materials for decision, discrimination to decide, and when he has decided, firmness and self-control to hold to his deliberate decision. And these qualities he requires and exercises exactly in proportion as the part of his conduct which he determines according to his own judgement and feelings is a large one. It is possible that he might be guided in some good path, and kept out of harm's way, without any of these things. But what will be his comparative worth as a human being? It really is of importance, not only what men do, but also what manner of men they are that do it. Among the works of man which human life is rightly employed in perfecting and beautifying, the first in importance surely is man himself. Supposing it were possible to get houses built, corn grown, battles fought, causes tried, and even churches erected and prayers said by machinery – by automatons in human form – it would be a considerable loss to exchange for these automatons even the men and women who at present inhabit the more civilized parts of the world, and who assuredly are but starved specimens of what nature can and will produce. Human nature is not a machine to be built after a model, and set to do exactly the work prescribed for it, but a tree, which requires to grow and develop itself on all sides, according to the tendency of the inward forces which make it a living thing.

It will probably be conceded that it is desirable people should exercise their understandings, and that an intelligent following of custom, or even occasionally an intelligent deviation from custom, is better than a blind and simply mechanical adhesion to it. To a certain extent it is admitted that our understanding should be our own; but there is not the same willingness to admit that our desires and impulses should be our own likewise, or that to possess impulses of our own, and of any strength, is anything but a peril and a snare. Yet desires and impulses are as much a part of a perfect human being as beliefs and restraints; and strong impulses are only perilous when not properly balanced, when one set of aims and inclinations is developed into strength, while others, which ought to coexist with them, remain weak and inactive. It is not because men's desires are strong that they act ill; it is because their consciences are weak. There is no natural connection between strong impulses and a weak conscience. The natural connection is the other way. To say that one person's desires and feelings are stronger and more various than those of another is merely to say that he has more of the raw material of human nature and is therefore capable, perhaps of more evil, but certainly of more good. Strong impulses are but another name for energy. Energy may be turned to bad uses; but more good may always be made of an energetic nature than of an indolent and impassive one. Those who have most natural feeling are always those whose cultivated feelings may be made the strongest. The same strong susceptibilities which make the personal impulses vivid and powerful are also the source from whence are generated the most passionate love of virtue and the sternest self-control. It is through the cultivation of these that society both does its duty and protects its interests, not by rejecting the stuff of which heroes are made, because it knows not how to make them. A person whose desires and impulses are his own – are the expression of his own nature, as it has been developed and modified by his own culture – is said to have a character. One whose desires and impulses are not his own has no character, no more than a steam engine has a character. If, in addition to being his own, his impulses are strong and are under the government of a strong will, he has an energetic character. Whoever thinks that individuality of desires and impulses should not be encouraged to unfold itself must maintain that society has no need of strong natures – is not the better for containing many persons who have much character – and that a high general average of energy is not desirable.

In some early states of society, these forces might be, and were, too much ahead of the power which society then possessed of disciplining and controlling them. There has been a time when the element of spontaneity and individuality was in excess, and the social principle had a hard struggle with it. The difficulty then was to induce men of strong bodies or minds to pay obedience to any rules which required them to control their impulses. To overcome this difficulty, law and discipline, like the Popes struggling against the Emperors, asserted a power over the whole man, claiming to control all his life in order to control his character – which society had not found any other sufficient means of binding. But society has now fairly got the better of individuality; and the danger which threatens human nature is not the excess, but the deficiency, of personal impulses and preferences. Things are vastly changed since the passions of those who were strong by station or by personal endowment were in a state of habitual rebellion against laws and ordinances, and required to be rigorously chained up to enable the persons within their reach to enjoy any particle of security. In our times, from the highest class of society down to the lowest, everyone lives as under the eye of a hostile and dreaded censorship. Not only in what concerns others, but in what concerns only themselves, the individual or the family do not ask themselves, what do I prefer? or, what would suit my character and disposition? or, what would allow the best and highest in me to have fair play and enable it to grow and thrive? They ask themselves, what is suitable to my position? what is usually done by persons of my station and pecuniary circumstances? or (worse still) what is usually done by persons of a station and circumstances superior to mine? I do not mean that they choose what is customary in preference to what suits their own inclination. It does not occur to them to have any inclination except for what is customary. Thus the mind itself is bowed to the yoke: even in what people do for pleasure, conformity is the first thing thought of; they like in crowds; they exercise choice only among things commonly done; peculiarity of taste, eccentricity of conduct are shunned equally with crimes, until by dint of not following their own nature they have no nature to follow: their human capacities are withered and starved; they become incapable of any strong wishes or native pleasures, and are generally without either opinions or feelings of home growth, or properly their own. Now is this, or is it not, the desirable condition of human nature?

It is so, on the Calvinistic theory. According to that, the one great offence of man is self-will. All the good of which humanity is capable is comprised in obedience. You have no choice; thus you must do, and no otherwise: 'Whatever is not a duty is a sin.' Human nature being radically corrupt, there is no redemption for anyone until human nature is killed within him. To one holding this theory of life, crushing out any of the human faculties, capacities, and susceptibilities is no evil: man needs no capacity but that of surrendering himself to the will of God; and if he uses any of his faculties for any other purpose but to do that supposed will more effectually, he is better without them. This is the theory of Calvinism; and it is held, in a mitigated form, by many who do not consider themselves Calvinists; the mitigation consisting in giving a less ascetic interpretation to the alleged will of God, asserting it to be his will that mankind should gratify some of their inclinations; of course not in the manner they themselves prefer, but in the way of obedience, that is, in a way prescribed to them by authority; and, therefore, by the necessary condition of the case, the same for all.

In some such insidious form there is at present a strong tendency to this narrow theory of life, and to the pinched and hidebound type of human character which it patronizes. Many persons, no doubt, sincerely think that human beings thus cramped and dwarfed are as their Maker designed them to be, just as many have thought that trees are a much finer thing when clipped into pollards, or cut out into figures of animals, than as nature made them. But if it be any part of religion to believe that man was made by a good Being, it is more consistent with that faith to believe that this Being gave all human faculties that they might be cultivated and unfolded, not rooted out and consumed, and that he takes delight in every nearer approach made by his creatures to the ideal conception embodied in them, every increase in any of their capabilities of comprehension, of action, or of enjoyment. There is a different type of human excellence from the Calvinistic: a conception of humanity as having its nature bestowed on it for other purposes than merely to be abnegated. 'Pagan self-assertion' is one of the elements of human worth, as well as 'Christian self-denial'.* There is a Greek ideal of self-development, which the Platonic and Christian ideal of self-government blends with, but does not supersede. It may be better to be a John Knox than an Alcibiades, but it is better to be a Pericles than either; nor would a Pericles, if we had one in these days, be without anything good which belonged to John Knox.[19]

It is not by wearing down into uniformity all that is individual in themselves, but by cultivating it and calling it forth, within the limits imposed by the rights and interests of others, that human beings become a noble and beautiful object of contemplation; and as the works partake the character of those who do them, by the same process human life also becomes rich, diversified, and animating, furnishing more abundant aliment to high thoughts and elevating feelings, and strengthening the tie which binds every individual to the race, by making the race infinitely better worth belonging to. In proportion to the development of his individuality, each person becomes more valuable to himself, and is, therefore, capable of being more valuable to others. There is a greater fullness of life about his own existence, and when there is more

---

* Sterling's *Essays*. [John Sterling, *Essays and Tales*, ed. Julius Hare, London, 1848, vol. I, p. 190.

19. To Mill, Knox represented the one extreme of rigid self-control and self-abnegation, and Alcibiades the other, wilful passion and self-interest. Pericles, of course, epitomized the ideal synthesis of virtues.

life in the units there is more in the mass which is composed of them. As much compression as is necessary to prevent the stronger specimens of human nature from encroaching on the rights of others cannot be dispensed with; but for this there is ample compensation even in the point of view of human development. The means of development which the individual loses by being prevented from gratifying his inclinations to the injury of others are chiefly obtained at the expense of the development of other people. And even to himself there is a full equivalent in the better development of the social part of his nature, rendered possible by the restraint put upon the selfish part. To be held to rigid rules of justice for the sake of others, develops the feelings and capacities which have the good of others for their object. But to be restrained in things not affecting their good, by their mere displeasure, develops nothing valuable except such force of character as may unfold itself in resisting the restraint. If acquiesced in, it dulls and blunts the whole nature. To give any fair play to the nature of each, it is essential that different persons should be allowed to lead different lives. In proportion as this latitude has been exercised in any age has that age been noteworthy to posterity. Even despotism does not produce its worst effects so long as individuality exists under it; and whatever crushes individuality is despotism, by whatever name it may be called and whether it professes to be enforcing the will of God or the injunctions of men.

Having said that the individuality is the same thing with development, and that it is only the cultivation of individuality which produces, or can produce, well-developed human beings, I might here close the argument; for what more or better can be said of any condition of human affairs than that it brings human beings themselves nearer to the best thing they can be? Or what worse can be said of any obstruction to good than that it prevents this? Doubtless, however, these considerations will not suffice to convince those who most need convincing; and it is necessary further to show that these developed human beings are of some use to the undeveloped – to point out to those who do not desire liberty, and would not avail themselves of it, that they may be in some intelligible manner rewarded for allowing other people to make use of it without hindrance.

In the first place, then, I would suggest that they might possibly learn something from them. It will not be denied by anybody that originality is a valuable element in human affairs. There is always need of persons not only to discover new truths and point out when what were once truths are true no longer, but also to commence new practices and set the example of more enlightened conduct and better taste and sense in human life. This cannot well be gainsaid by anybody who does not believe that the world has already attained perfection in all its ways and practices. It is true that this benefit is not capable of being rendered by everybody alike; there are but few persons, in comparison with the whole of mankind, whose experiments, if adopted by others, would be likely to be any improvement on established practice. But these few are the salt of the earth; without them, human life would become a stagnant pool. Not only is it they who introduce good things which did not before exist; it is they who keep the life in those which already exist. If there were nothing new to be done, would human intellect cease to be necessary? Would it be a reason why those who do the old things should forget why they are done, and do them like cattle, not like human beings? There is only too great a tendency in the best beliefs and practices to degenerate into the mechanical; and unless there were a succession of persons whose ever-recurring originality prevents the grounds of those beliefs and practices from becoming merely traditional, such dead matter would not resist the smallest shock from anything really alive, and there would be no reason why civilization should not die out, as in the Byzantine Empire. Persons of genius, it is true, are, and are always likely to be, a small minority; but in order to have them, it is necessary to preserve the soil in which they grow. Genius can only breathe freely in an *atmosphere* of freedom. Persons of genius are, *ex vi termini*,[20] more individual than any other people – less capable, consequently, of fitting themselves,

20. By definition.

without hurtful compression, into any of the small number of moulds which society provides in order to save its members the trouble of forming their own character. If from timidity they consent to be forced into one of these moulds, and to let all that part of themselves which cannot expand under the pressure remain unexpanded, society will be little the better for their genius. If they are of a strong character and break their fetters, they become a mark for the society which has not succeeded in reducing them to commonplace, to point out with solemn warning as 'wild', 'erratic', and the like – much as if one should complain of the Niagara river for not flowing smoothly between its banks like a Dutch canal.

I insist thus emphatically on the importance of genius and the necessity of allowing it to unfold itself freely both in thought and in practice, being well aware that no one will deny the position in theory, but knowing also that almost everyone, in reality, is totally indifferent to it. People think genius a fine thing if it enables a man to write an exciting poem or paint a picture. But in its true sense, that of originality in thought and action, though no one says that it is not a thing to be admired, nearly all, at heart, think that they can do very well without it. Unhappily this is too natural to be wondered at. Originality is the one thing which unoriginal minds cannot feel the use of. They cannot see what it is to do for them: how should they? If they could see what it would do for them, it would not be originality. The first service which originality has to render them is that of opening their eyes: which being once fully done, they would have a chance of being themselves original. Meanwhile, recollecting that nothing was ever done which someone was not the first to do, and that all good things which exist are the fruits of originality, let them be modest enough to believe that there is something still left for it to accomplish, and assure themselves that they are more in need of originality, the less they are conscious of the want.

In sober truth, whatever homage may be professed, or even paid, to real or supposed mental superiority, the general tendency of things throughout the world is to render mediocrity the ascendant power among mankind. In ancient history, in the Middle Ages, and in a diminishing degree through the long transition from feudality to the present time, the individual was a power in himself; and if he had either great talents or a high social position, he was a considerable power. At present individuals are lost in the crowd. In politics it is almost a triviality to say that public opinion now rules the world. The only power deserving the name is that of masses, and of governments while they make themselves the organ of the tendencies and instincts of masses. This is as true in the moral and social relations of private life as in public transactions. Those whose opinions go by the name of public opinion are not always the same sort of public: in America, they are the whole white population; in England, chiefly the middle class. But they are always a mass, that is to say, collective mediocrity. And what is a still greater novelty, the mass do not now take their opinions from dignitaries in Church or State, from ostensible leaders, or from books. Their thinking is done for them by men much like themselves, addressing them or speaking in their name, on the spur of the moment, through the newspapers. I am not complaining of all this. I do not assert that anything better is compatible, as a general rule, with the present low state of the human mind. But that does not hinder the government of mediocrity from being mediocre government. No government by a democracy or a numerous aristocracy, either in its political acts or in the opinions, qualities, and tone of mind which it fosters, ever did or could rise above mediocrity except in so far as the sovereign many have let themselves be guided (which in their best times they always have done) by the counsels and influence of a more highly gifted and instructed *one* or *few*. The initiation of all wise or noble things comes and must come from individuals; generally at first from some one individual. The honour and glory of the average man is that he is capable of following that initiative; that he can respond internally to wise and noble things, and be led to them with his eyes open. I am not countenancing the sort of 'hero-worship' which applauds the strong man of genius for forcibly seizing on the government of the world and making it do his bidding in spite of itself.[21] All he can claim is freedom to point out the way. The power of compelling others into it is not only inconsistent with the freedom and development of all the rest, but corrupting to the strong man himself. It does seem, however, that when the opinions of masses of merely average men are everywhere become or becoming the dominant power, the counterpoise and corrective to that tendency would be the more and more pronounced individuality of those who stand on the higher eminences of thought. It is in these circumstances most especially that exceptional individuals, instead of being deterred, should be encouraged in acting differently from the mass. In other times there was no advantage in their doing so, unless they acted not only differently but better. In this age, the mere example of non-conformity, the mere refusal to bend the knee to custom, is itself a service. Precisely because the tyranny of opinion is such as to make eccentricity a reproach, it is desirable, in order to break through that tyranny, that people should be eccentric. Eccentricity has always abounded when and where strength of character has abounded; and the amount of eccentricity in a society has generally been proportional to the amount of genius, mental vigour, and moral courage it contained. That so few now dare to be eccentric marks the chief danger of the time.

I have said that it is important to give the freest scope possible to uncustomary things, in order that it may in time appear which of these are fit to be converted into customs. But independence of action and disregard of custom are not solely deserving of encouragement for the chance they afford that better modes of action, and customs more worthy of general adoption, may be struck out; nor is it only persons of decided mental superiority who have a just claim to carry on their lives in their own way. There is no reason that all human existence should be constructed on some one or some small number of patterns. If a person possesses any tolerable amount

21. Probably a reference to Carlyle's *On Heroes, Hero-Worship, and the Heroic in History* (1841).

of common sense and experience, his own mode of laying out his existence is the best, not because it is the best in itself, but because it is his own mode. Human beings are not like sheep; and even sheep are not undistinguishably alike. A man cannot get a coat or a pair of boots to fit him unless they are either made to his measure or he has a whole warehouseful to choose from; and is it easier to fit him with a life than with a coat, or are human beings more like one another in their whole physical and spiritual conformation than in the shape of their feet? If it were only that people have diversities of taste, that is reason enough for not attempting to shape them all after one model. But different persons also require different conditions for their spiritual development; and can no more exist healthily in the same moral, than all the variety of plants can in the same physical, atmosphere and climate. The same things which are helps to one person towards the cultivation of his higher nature are hindrances to another. The same mode of life is a healthy excitement to one, keeping all his faculties of action and enjoyment in their best order, while to another it is a distracting burden which suspends or crushes all internal life. Such are the differences among human beings in their sources of pleasure, their susceptibilities of pain, and the operation on them of different physical and moral agencies that, unless there is a corresponding diversity in their modes of life, they neither obtain their fair share of happiness, nor grow up to the mental, moral, and aesthetic stature of which their nature is capable. Why then should tolerance, as far as the public sentiment is concerned, extend only to tastes and modes of life which extort acquiescence by the multitude of their adherents? Nowhere (except in some monastic institutions) is diversity of taste entirely unrecognized; a person may, without blame, either like or dislike rowing, or smoking, or music, or athletic exercises, or chess, or cards, or study, because both those who like each of these things and those who dislike them are too numerous to be put down. But the man, and still more the woman, who can be accused either of doing 'what nobody does', or of not doing 'what everybody does', is the subject of as much depreciatory remark as if he or she had committed some grave moral delinquency. Persons require to possess a title, or some other badge of rank, or of the consideration of people of rank, to be able to indulge somewhat in the luxury of doing as they like without detriment to their estimation. To indulge somewhat, I repeat: for whoever allow themselves much of that indulgence incur the risk of something worse than disparaging speeches – they are in peril of a commission *de lunatico* and of having their property taken from them and given to their relations.*

There is one characteristic of the present direction of public opinion peculiarly calculated to make it intolerant of any marked demonstrations of individuality. The general average of mankind are not only moderate in intellect, but also moderate in inclinations; they have no tastes or wishes strong enough to incline them to do anything unusual, and they consequently do not understand those who have, and class all such with the wild and intemperate whom they are accustomed to look down upon. Now, in addition to this fact

* There is something both contemptible and frightful in the sort of evidence on which, of late years, any person can be judicially declared unfit for the management of his affairs; and after his death, his disposal of his property can be set aside if there is enough of it to pay the expenses of litigation – which are charged on the property itself. All the minute details of his daily life are pried into, and whatever is found which, seen through the medium of the perceiving and describing faculties of the lowest of the low, bears an appearance unlike absolute commonplace, is laid before the jury as evidence of insanity, and often with success; the jurors being little, if at all, less vulgar and ignorant than the witnesses, while the judges, with that extraordinary want of knowledge of human nature and life which continually astonishes us in English lawyers, often help to mislead them. These trials speak volumes as to the state of feeling and opinion among the vulgar with regard to human liberty. So far from setting any value on individuality – so far from respecting the right of each individual to act, in things indifferent, as seems good to his own judgement and inclinations, judges and juries cannot even conceive that a person in a state of sanity can desire such freedom. In former days, when it was proposed to burn atheists, charitable people used to suggest putting them in a madhouse instead; it would be nothing surprising nowadays were we to see this done, and the doers applauding themselves because, instead of persecuting for religion, they had adopted so humane and Christian a mode of treating these unfortunates, not without a silent satisfaction at their having thereby obtained their deserts.

which is general, we have only to suppose that a strong movement has set in towards the improvement of morals, and it is evident what we have to expect. In these days such a movement has set in; much has actually been effected in the way of increased regularity of conduct and discouragement of excesses; and there is a philanthropic spirit abroad for the exercise of which there is no more inviting field than the moral and prudential improvement of our fellow creatures. These tendencies of the times cause the public to be more disposed than at most former periods to prescribe general rules of conduct and endeavour to make everyone conform to the approved standard. And that standard, express or tacit, is to desire nothing strongly. Its ideal of character is to be without any marked character – to maim by compression, like a Chinese lady's foot, every part of human nature which stands out prominently and tends to make the person markedly dissimilar in outline to commonplace humanity.

As is usually the case with ideals which exclude one-half of what is desirable, the present standard of approbation produces only an inferior imitation of the other half. Instead of great energies guided by vigorous reason, and strong feelings strongly controlled by a conscientious will, its result is weak feelings and weak energies, which therefore can be kept in outward conformity to rule without any strength either of will or of reason. Already energetic characters on any large scale are becoming merely traditional. There is now scarcely any outlet for energy in this country except business. The energy expended in this may still be regarded as considerable. What little is left from that employment is expended on some hobby, which may be a useful, even a philanthropic, hobby, but is always some one thing, and generally a thing of small dimensions. The greatness of England is now all collective; individually small, we only appear capable of anything great by our habit of combining; and with this our moral and religious philanthropists are perfectly contented. But it was men of another stamp than this that made England what it has been; and men of another stamp will be needed to prevent its decline.

The despotism of custom is everywhere the standing hindrance to human advancement, being in unceasing antagonism to that disposition to aim at something better than customary, which is called, according to circumstances, the spirit of liberty, or that of progress or improvement. The spirit of improvement is not always a spirit of liberty, for it may aim at forcing improvements on an unwilling people; and the spirit of liberty, in so far as it resists such attempts, may ally itself locally and temporarily with the opponents of improvement; but the only unfailing and permanent source of improvement is liberty, since by it there are as many possible independent centres of improvement as there are individuals. The progressive principle, however, in either shape, whether as the love of liberty or of improvement, is antagonistic to the sway of custom, involving at least emancipation from that yoke; and the contest between the two constitutes the chief interest of the history of mankind. The greater part of the world has, properly speaking, no history, because the despotism of custom is complete. This is the case over the whole East. Custom is there, in all things, the final appeal; justice and right mean conformity to custom; the argument of custom no one, unless some tyrant intoxicated with power, thinks of resisting. And we see the result. Those nations must once have had originality; they did not start out of the ground populous, lettered, and versed in many of the arts of life; they made themselves all this, and were then the greatest and most powerful nations of the world. What are they now? The subjects or dependants of tribes whose forefathers wandered in the forests when theirs had magnificent palaces and gorgeous temples, but over whom custom exercised only a divided rule with liberty and progress. A people, it appears, may be progressive for a certain length of time, and then stop: when does it stop? When it ceases to possess individuality. If a similar change should befall the nations of Europe, it will not be in exactly the same shape: the despotism of custom with which these nations are threatened is not precisely stationariness. It proscribes singularity, but it does not preclude change, provided all change together. We have discarded the fixed costumes of our forefathers; everyone must still dress like other people, but the fashion may change once or twice a year. We thus take care that when there is a change, it shall be for change's sake, and not from any idea of beauty or convenience; for the same idea of beauty or convenience would not strike all the world at the same moment, and be simultaneously thrown aside by all at another moment. But we are progressive as well as changeable: we continually make new inventions in mechanical things, and keep them until they are again superseded by better; we are eager for improvement in politics, in education, even in morals, though in this last our idea of improvement chiefly consists in persuading or forcing other people to be as good as ourselves. It is not progress that we object to; on the contrary, we flatter ourselves that we are the most progressive people who ever lived. It is individuality that we war against: we should think we had done wonders if we had made ourselves all alike, forgetting that the unlikeness of one person to another is generally the first thing which draws the attention of either to the imperfection of his own type and the superiority of another, or the possibility, by combining the advantages of both, of producing something better than either. We have a warning example in China – a nation of much talent and, in some respects, even wisdom, owing to the rare good fortune of having been provided at an early period with a particularly good set of customs, the work, in some measure, of men to whom even the most enlightened European must accord, under certain limitations, the title of sages and philosophers. They are remarkable, too, in the excellence of their apparatus for impressing, as far as possible, the best wisdom they possess upon every mind in the community, and securing that those who have appropriated most of it shall occupy the posts of honour and power. Surely the people who did this have discovered the secret of human progressiveness and must have kept themselves steadily at the head of the movement of the world. On the contrary, they have become stationary – have remained so for thousands of years; and if they are ever to be further improved, it must be by foreigners. They have succeeded beyond all hope in what English philanthropists are so industriously working at – in making a people all alike, all governing their thoughts and conduct by the same maxims and rules; and these are the fruits. The modern *régime* of public opinion is, in an unorganized form, what the Chinese educational and political systems are in an organized; and unless individuality shall be able successfully to assert itself against this yoke, Europe, notwithstanding its noble antecedents and its professed Christianity, will tend to become another China.

What is it that has hitherto preserved Europe from this lot? What has made the European family of nations an improving, instead of a stationary, portion of mankind? Not any superior excellence in them, which, when it exists, exists as the effect, not as the cause, but their remarkable diversity of character and culture. Individuals, classes, nations have been extremely unlike one another: they have struck out a great variety of paths, each leading to something valuable; and although at every period those who travelled in different paths have been intolerant of one another, and each would have thought it an excellent thing if all the rest could have been compelled to travel his road, their attempts to thwart each other's development have rarely had any permanent success, and each has in time endured to receive the good which the others have offered. Europe is, in my judgement, wholly indebted to this plurality of paths for its progressive and many-sided development. But it already begins to possess this benefit in a considerably less degree. It is decidedly advancing towards the Chinese ideal of making all people alike. M. de Tocqueville, in his last important work, remarks how much more the Frenchmen of the present day resemble one another than did those even of the last generation.[22] The same remark might be made of Englishmen in a far greater degree. In a passage already quoted from Wilhelm von

22. Tocqueville's *L'Ancien Régime et La Révolution* was published in France in 1856 and translated into English the same year. Chapter viii of Part II was entitled, 'How France had become the country in which men were most like each other'.

Humboldt,[23] he points out two things as necessary conditions of human development – because necessary to render people unlike one another – namely, freedom and variety of situations. The second of these two conditions is in this country every day diminishing. The circumstances which surround different classes and individuals, and shape their characters, are daily becoming more assimilated. Formerly, different ranks, different neighbourhoods, different trades and professions lived in what might be called different worlds; at present, to a great degree in the same. Comparatively speaking, they now read the same things, listen to the same things, see the same things, go to the same places, have their hopes and fears directed to the same objects, have the same rights and liberties, and the same means of asserting them. Great as are the differences of position which remain, they are nothing to those which have ceased. And the assimilation is still proceeding. All the political changes of the age promote it, since they all tend to raise the low and to lower the high. Every extension of education promotes it, because education brings people under common influences and gives them access to the general stock of facts and sentiments. Improvement in the means of communication promotes it, by bringing the inhabitants of distant places into personal contact, and keeping up a rapid flow of changes of residence between one place and another. The increase of commerce and manufactures promotes it, by diffusing more widely the advantages of easy circumstances and opening all objects of ambition, even the highest, to general competition, whereby the desire of rising becomes no longer the character of a particular class, but of all classes. A more powerful agency than even all these, in bringing about a general similarity among mankind, is the complete establishment, in this and other free countries, of the ascendancy of public opinion in the State. As the various social eminences which enabled persons entrenched on them to disregard the opinion of the multitude gradually become levelled; as the very idea of resisting the will of the public, when it is positively known that they have a will, disappears more and more

23. See above, pp. 121

from the minds of practical politicians, there ceases to be any social support for nonconformity – any substantive power in society which, itself opposed to the ascendancy of numbers, is interested in taking under its protection opinions and tendencies at variance with those of the public.

The combination of all these causes forms so great a mass of influences hostile to individuality that it is not easy to see how it can stand its ground. It will do so with increasing difficulty unless the intelligent part of the public can be made to feel its value – to see that it is good there should be differences, even though not for the better, even though, as it may appear to them, some should be for the worse. If the claims of individuality are ever to be asserted, the time is now, while much is still wanting to complete the enforced assimilation. It is only in the earlier stages that any stand can be successfully made against the encroachment. The demand that all other people shall resemble ourselves grows by what it feeds on. If resistance waits till life is reduced *nearly* to one uniform type, all deviations from that type will come to be considered impious, immoral, even monstrous and contrary to nature. Mankind speedily become unable to conceive diversity when they have been for some time unaccustomed to see it.

CHAPTER IV

*Of the Limits to the
Authority of Society
over the Individual*

WHAT, then, is the rightful limit to the sovereignty of the individual over himself? Where does the authority of society begin? How much of human life should be assigned to individuality, and how much to society?

Each will receive its proper share if each has that which more particularly concerns it. To individuality should belong the part of life in which it is chiefly the individual that is interested; to society, the part which chiefly interests society.

Though society is not founded on a contract, and though no good purpose is answered by inventing a contract in order to deduce social obligations from it, everyone who receives the protection of society owes a return for the benefit, and the fact of living in society renders it indispensable that each should be bound to observe a certain line of conduct towards the rest. This conduct consists, first, in not injuring the interests of one another, or rather certain interests which, either by express legal provision or by tacit understanding, ought to be considered as rights; and secondly, in each person's bearing his share (to be fixed on some equitable principle) of the labours and sacrifices incurred for defending the society or its members from injury and molestation. These conditions society is justified in enforcing at all costs to those who endeavour to withhold fulfilment. Nor is this all that society may do. The acts of an individual may be hurtful to others or wanting in due consideration for their welfare, without going to the length of violating any of their constituted rights. The offender may then be justly punished by opinion, though not by law. As soon as any part of a person's conduct affects prejudicially the interests of others, society has jurisdiction over it, and the question whether the general welfare will or will not be promoted by interfering with it becomes open to discussion. But there is no room for entertaining any such question when a person's conduct affects the interests of no persons besides himself, or needs not affect them unless they like (all the persons concerned being of full age and the ordinary amount of understanding). In all such cases, there should be perfect freedom, legal and social, to do the action and stand the consequences.

It would be a great misunderstanding of this doctrine to suppose that it is one of selfish indifference which pretends that human beings have no business with each other's conduct in life, and that they should not concern themselves about the well-doing or well-being of one another, unless their own interest is involved. Instead of any diminution, there is need of a great increase of disinterested exertion to promote the good of others. But disinterested benevolence can find other instruments to persuade people to their good than whips and scourges, either of the literal or the metaphorical sort. I am the last person to undervalue the self-regarding virtues; they are only second in importance, if even second, to the social. It is equally the business of education to cultivate both. But even education works by conviction and persuasion as well as by compulsion, and it is by the former only that, when the period of education is passed, the self-regarding virtues should be inculcated. Human beings owe to each other help to distinguish the better from the worse, and encouragement to choose the former and avoid the latter. They should be forever stimulating each other to increased exercise of their higher faculties and increased direction of their feelings and aims towards wise instead of foolish, elevating instead of degrading, objects and contemplations. But neither one person, nor any number of persons, is warranted in saying to another human creature of ripe years that he shall not do with his life for his own benefit what he chooses to do with it. He is the person most interested in his own well-being: the interest which any other person, except in cases of strong personal attachment, can have in it is trifling compared with that which he himself has; the interest which society has in him individually (except as to his conduct to others) is fractional and altogether indirect, while with respect to his own feelings and circumstances the most ordinary man or woman has means of knowledge immeasurably surpassing those that can be possessed by anyone else. The interference of society to overrule his judgement and purposes in what only regards himself must be grounded on general presumptions which may be altogether wrong and, even if right, are as likely as not to be misapplied to individual cases, by persons no better acquainted with the circumstances of such cases than those are who look at them merely from without. In this department, therefore, of human affairs, individuality has its proper field of action. In the conduct of human beings towards one another it is necessary that general rules should for the most part be observed in order that people may know what they have to expect; but in each person's own concerns his individual spontaneity is entitled to free exercise. Considerations to aid his judgement, exhortations to strengthen his will, may be offered to him, even obtruded on him, by others; but he himself is the final judge. All errors which he is likely to commit against advice and warning are far outweighed by the evil of allowing others to constrain him to what they deem his good.

I do not mean that the feelings with which a person is regarded by others ought not to be in any way affected by his self-regarding qualities or deficiencies. This is neither possible nor desirable. If he is eminent in any of the qualities which conduce to his own good, he is, so far, a proper object of admiration. He is so much the nearer to the ideal perfection of human nature. If he is grossly deficient in those qualities, a sentiment the opposite of admiration will follow. There is a degree of folly, and a degree of what may be called (though the phrase is not unobjectionable) lowness or depravation of taste, which, though it cannot justify doing harm to the person who manifests it, renders him necessarily and properly a subject of distate, or, in extreme cases, even of contempt: a person could not have the opposite qualities in due strength without entertaining these feelings. Though doing no wrong to anyone, a person may so act as to compel us to judge him, and feel to him, as a fool or as a being of an inferior order; and since this judgement and feeling are a fact which he would prefer to avoid, it is doing him a service to warn him of it beforehand, as of any other disagreeable consequence to which he exposes himself. It would be well, indeed, if this good office were much more freely rendered than the common notions of politeness at present permit, and if one person could honestly point out to another that he thinks him in fault, without being considered unmannerly or presuming. We have a right, also, in various ways, to act upon our unfavourable opinion of anyone, not to the oppression of his individuality, but in the exercise of ours. We are not bound, for example, to seek his society; we have a right to avoid it (though not to parade the avoidance), for we have a right to choose the society most acceptable to us. We have a right, and it may be our duty, to caution others against him if we think his example or conversation likely to have a pernicious effect on those with whom he associates. We may give others a preference over him in optional good offices, except those which tend to his improvement. In these various modes a person may suffer very severe penalties at the hands of others for faults which directly concern only himself; but he suffers these penalties only in so far as they are the natural and, as it were, the spontaneous consequences of the faults themselves, not because they are purposely inflicted on him for the sake of punishment. A person who shows rashness, obstinacy, self-conceit – who cannot live within moderate means; who cannot restrain himself from hurtful indulgence; who pursues animal pleasures at the expense of those of feeling and intellect – must expect to be lowered in the opinion of others, and to have a less share of their favourable sentiments; but of this he has no right to complain unless he has merited their favour by special excellence in his social relations and has thus established a title to their good offices, which is not affected by his demerits towards himself.

What I contend for is that the inconveniences which are strictly inseparable from the unfavourable judgement of others are the only ones to which a person should ever be subjected for that portion of his conduct and character which concerns his own good, but which does not affect the interest of others in their relations with him. Acts injurious to others require a totally different treatment. Encroachment on their rights; infliction on them of any loss or damage not justified by his own rights; falsehood or duplicity in dealing with them; unfair or ungenerous use of advantages over them; even selfish abstinence from defending them against injury – these are fit objects of moral reprobation and, in grave cases, of moral retribution and punishment. And not only these acts, but the dispositions which lead to them, are properly immoral and fit subjects of disapprobation which may rise to abhorrence. Cruelty of disposition; malice and ill-nature; that most antisocial and odious of all passions, envy; dissimulation and insincerity, irascibility on insufficient cause, and resentment disproportioned to the provocation; the love of domineering over others; the desire to engross more than one's share of advantages (the πλεονεχια of the Greeks),[24] the pride which derives gratification from the abasement of others; the egotism which thinks self and its concerns more important than everything else, and decides all doubtful questions in its own favour – these are moral vices and constitute a bad and odious moral character; unlike the self-regarding faults previously mentioned, which are not properly immoralities and, to whatever pitch they may be carried, do not constitute wickedness. They may be proofs of any amount of folly or want of personal dignity and self-respect, but they are only a subject of moral reprobation when they involve a breach of duty to others, for whose sake the individual is bound to have care for himself. What are called duties to ourselves are not socially obligatory unless circumstances render them at the same time duties to others. The term duty to oneself, when it means anything more than prudence, means self-respect or self-development, and for none of these is anyone accountable to his fellow creatures, because for none of them is it for the good of mankind that he be held accountable to them.

The distinction between the loss of consideration which a person may rightly incur by defect of prudence or of personal

24. πλεονεχια – the desire to engross.

dignity, and the reprobation which is due to him for an offence against the rights of others, is not a merely nominal distinction. It makes a vast difference both in our feelings and in our conduct towards him whether he displeases us in things in which we think we have a right to control him or in things in which we know that we have not. If he displeases us, we may express our distaste, and we may stand aloof from a person as well as from a thing that displeases us; but we shall not therefore feel called on to make his life uncomfortable. We shall reflect that he already bears, or will bear, the whole penalty of his error; if he spoils his life by mismanagement, we shall not, for that reason, desire to spoil it still further; instead of wishing to punish him, we shall rather endeavour to alleviate his punishment by showing him how he may avoid or cure the evils his conduct tends to bring upon him. He may be to us an object of pity, perhaps of dislike, but not of anger or resentment; we shall not treat him like an enemy of society; the worst we shall think ourselves justified in doing is leaving him to himself, if we do not interfere benevolently by showing interest or concern for him. It is far otherwise if he has infringed the rules necessary for the protection of his fellow creatures, individually or collectively. The evil consequences of his acts do not then fall on himself, but on others; and society, as the protector of all its members, must retaliate on him, must inflict pain on him for the express purpose of punishment, and must take care that it be sufficiently severe. In the one case, he is an offender at our bar, and we are called on not only to sit in judgment on him, but, in one shape or another, to execute our own sentence; in the other case, it is not our part to inflict any suffering on him, except what may incidentally follow from our using the same liberty in the regulation of our own affairs which we allow to him in his.

The distinction here pointed out between the part of a person's life which concerns only himself and that which concerns others, many persons will refuse to admit. How (it may be asked) can any part of the conduct of a member of society be a matter of indifference to the other members? No person is an entirely isolated being; it is impossible for a person to do anything seriously or permanently hurtful to himself without mischief reaching at least to his near connections, and often far beyond them. If he injures his property, he does harm to those who directly or indirectly derived support from it, and usually diminishes, by a greater or less amount, the general resources of the community. If he deteriorates his bodily or mental faculties, he not only brings evil upon all who depended on him for any portion of their happiness, but disqualifies himself for rendering the services which he owes to his fellow creatures generally, perhaps becomes a burden on their affection or benevolence; and if such conduct were very frequent hardly any offence that is committed would detract more from the general sum of good. Finally, if by his vices or follies a person does no direct harm to others, he is nevertheless (it may be said) injurious by his example, and ought to be compelled to control himself for the sake of those whom the sight or knowledge of his conduct might corrupt or mislead.

And even (it will be added) if the consequences of misconduct could be confined to the vicious or thoughtless individual, ought society to abandon to their own guidance those who are manifestly unfit for it? If protection against themselves is confessedly due to children and persons under age, is not society equally bound to afford it to persons of mature years who are equally incapable of self-government? If gambling, or drunkenness, or incontinence, or idleness, or uncleanliness are as injurious to happiness, and as great a hindrance to improvement, as many or most of the acts prohibited by law, why (it may be asked) should not law, so far as is consistent with practicability and social convenience, endeavour to repress these also? And as a supplement to the unavoidable imperfections of law, ought not opinion at least to organize a powerful police against these vices and visit rigidly with social penalties those who are known to practise them? There is no question here (it may be said) about restricting individuality, or impeding the trial of new and original experiments in living. The only things it is sought to prevent are things which have been tried and condemned from the beginning of the world until now – things which experience has shown not to be useful or suitable to any person's individuality. There must be some length of time and amount of experience after which a moral or prudential truth may be regarded as established; and it is merely desired to prevent generation after generation from falling over the same precipice which has been fatal to their predecessors.

I fully admit that the mischief which a person does to himself may seriously affect, both through their sympathies and their interests, those nearly connected with him and, in a minor degree, society at large. When, by conduct of this sort, a person is led to violate a distinct and assignable obligation to any other person or persons, the case is taken out of the self-regarding class and becomes amenable to moral disapprobation in the proper sense of the term. If, for example, a man, through intemperance or extravagance, becomes unable to pay his debts, or, having undertaken the moral responsibility of a family, becomes from the same cause incapable of supporting or educating them, he is deservedly reprobated and might be justly punished; but it is for the breach of duty to his family or creditor, not for the extravagance. If the resources which ought to have been devoted to them had been diverted from them for the most prudent investment, the moral culpability would have been the same. George Barnwell murdered his uncle to get money for his mistress, but if he had done it to set himself up in business, he would equally have been hanged.[25] Again, in the frequent case of a man who causes grief to his family by addiction to bad habits, he deserves reproach for his unkindness or ingratitude; but so he may for cultivating habits not in themselves vicious, if they are painful to those with whom he passes his life, or who from personal ties are dependent on him for

25. *The London Merchant, or The History of George Barnwell*, a play by George Lillo based on a popular ballad, was first produced at Drury Lane in 1731. Shown in various versions in the 18th and 19th centuries, it was also published as a short story in 1829. It was a morality play about a young apprentice of London who, under the corrupting influence of a woman of the town, was induced first to rob his master and then to murder his uncle.

their comfort. Whoever fails in the consideration generally due to the interests and feelings of others, not being compelled by some more imperative duty, or justified by allowable self-preference, is a subject of moral disapprobation for that failure, but not for the cause of it, nor for the errors, merely personal to himself, which may have remotely led to it. In like manner, when a person disables himself, by conduct purely self-regarding, from the performance of some definite duty incumbent on him to the public, he is guilty of a social offence. No person ought to be punished simply for being drunk; but a soldier or a policeman should be punished for being drunk on duty. Whenever, in short, there is a definite damage, or a definite risk of damage, either to an individual or to the public, the case is taken out of the province of liberty and placed in that of morality or law.

But with regard to the merely contingent or, as it may be called, constructive injury which a person causes to society by conduct which neither violates any specific duty to the public, nor occasions perceptible hurt to any assignable individual except himself, the inconvenience is one which society can afford to bear, for the sake of the greater good of human freedom. If grown persons are to be punished for not taking proper care of themselves, I would rather it were for their own sake than under pretence of preventing them from impairing their capacity or rendering to society benefits which society does not pretend it has a right to exact. But I cannot consent to argue the point as if society had no means of bringing its weaker members up to its ordinary standard of rational conduct, except waiting till they do something irrational, and then punishing them, legally or morally, for it. Society has had absolute power over them during all the early portion of their existence; it has had the whole period of childhood and nonage in which to try whether it could make them capable of rational conduct in life. The existing generation is master both of the training and the entire circumstances of the generation to come; it cannot indeed make them perfectly wise and good, because it is itself so lamentably deficient in goodness and wisdom; and its best efforts are not always, in individual cases, its most successful ones; but it is perfectly well able to make the rising generation, as a whole, as good as, and a little better than, itself. If society lets any considerable number of its members grow up mere children, incapable of being acted on by rational consideration of distant motives, society has itself to blame for the consequences. Armed not only with all the powers of education, but with the ascendancy which the authority of a received opinion always exercises over the minds who are least fitted to judge for themselves, and aided by the *natural* penalties which cannot be prevented from falling on those who incur the distaste or the contempt of those who know them – let not society pretend that it needs, besides all this, the power to issue commands and enforce obedience in the personal concerns of individuals in which, on all principles of justice and policy, the decision ought to rest with those who are to abide the consequences. Nor is there anything which tends more to discredit and frustrate the better means of influencing conduct than a resort to the worse. If there be among those whom it is attempted to coerce into prudence or temperance any of the material of which vigorous and independent characters are made, they will infallibly rebel against the yoke. No such person will ever feel that others have a right to control him in his concerns, such as they have to prevent him from injuring them in theirs; and it easily comes to be considered a mark of spirit and courage to fly in the face of such usurped authority and do with ostentation the exact opposite of what it enjoins, as in the fashion of grossness which succeeded, in the time of Charles II, to the fanatical moral intolerance of the Puritans. With respect to what is said of the necessity of protecting society from the bad example set to others by the vicious or the self-indulgent, it is true that bad example may have a pernicious effect, especially the example of doing wrong to others with impunity to the wrong-doer. But we are now speaking of conduct which, while it does no wrong to others, is supposed to do great harm to the agent himself; and I do not see how those who believe this can think otherwise than that the example, on the whole, must be more salutary than hurtful, since, if it displays the misconduct, it displays also the painful or degrading consequences which, if the conduct is justly censured, must be supposed to be in all or most cases attendant on it.

But the strongest of all the arguments against the interference of the public with purely personal conduct is that, when it does interfere, the odds are that it interferes wrongly and in the wrong place. On questions of social morality, of duty to others, the opinion of the public, that is, of an overruling majority, though often wrong, is likely to be still oftener right, because on such questions they are only required to judge of their own interests, of the manner in which some mode of conduct, if allowed to be practised, would affect themselves. But the opinion of a similar majority, imposed as a law on the minority, on questions of self-regarding conduct is quite as likely to be wrong as right, for in these cases public opinion means, at the best, some people's opinion of what is good or bad for other people, while very often it does not even mean that – the public, with the most perfect indifference, passing over the pleasure or convenience of those whose conduct they censure and considering only their own preference. There are many who consider as an injury to themselves any conduct which they have a distaste for, and resent it as an outrage to their feelings; as a religious bigot, when charged with disregarding the religious feelings of others, has been known to retort that they disregard his feelings by persisting in their abominable worship or creed. But there is no parity between the feeling of a person for his own opinion and the feeling of another who is offended at his holding it, no more than between the desire of a thief to take a purse and the desire of the right owner to keep it. And a person's taste is as much his own peculiar concern as his opinion or his purse. It is easy for anyone to imagine an ideal public which leaves the freedom and choice of individuals in all uncertain matters undisturbed and only requires them to abstain from modes of conduct which universal experience has condemned. But where has there been seen a public which set any such limit to its censorship? Or when does the public trouble itself about universal experience? In its interferences with personal conduct it is seldom thinking of anything but the enormity of acting or feeling differently from itself; and this standard of judgement, thinly disguised, is held up to mankind as the dictate of religion and philosophy by nine-tenths of all moralists and speculative writers. These teach that things are right because they are right; because we feel them to be so. They tell us to search in our own minds and hearts for laws of conduct binding on ourselves and on all others. What can the poor public do but apply these instructions and make their own personal feelings of good and evil, if they are tolerably unanimous in them, obligatory on all the world?

The evil here pointed out is not one which exists only in theory; and it may perhaps be expected that I should specify the instances in which the public of this age and country improperly invests its own preferences with the character of moral laws. I am not writing an essay on the aberrations of existing moral feeling. That is too weighty a subject to be discussed parenthetically, and by way of illustration. Yet examples are necessary to show that the principle I maintain is of serious and practical moment, and that I am not endeavouring to erect a barrier against imaginary evils. And it is not difficult to show, by abundant instances, that to extend the bounds of what may be called moral police until it encroaches on the most unquestionably legitimate liberty of the individual is one of the most universal of all human propensities.

As a first instance, consider the antipathies which men cherish on no better grounds than that persons whose religious opinions are different from theirs do not practise their religious observances, especially their religious abstinences. To cite a rather trivial example, nothing in the creed or practice of Christians does more to envenom the hatred of Mohammedans against them than the fact of their eating pork. There are few acts which Christians and Europeans regard with more unaffected disgust than Mussulmans[26] regard this particular mode of satisfying hunger. It is in the first place, an offence against their religion; but this circumstance by no means explains either the degree or the kind of

26. A common 19th century spelling for Moslems.

their repugnance; for wine also is forbidden by their religion: and to partake of it is by all Mussulmans accounted wrong, but not disgusting. Their aversion to the flesh of the 'unclean beast' is, on the contrary, of that peculiar character, resembling an instinctive antipathy, which the idea of uncleanness, when once it throughly sinks into the feelings, seems always to excite even in those whose personal habits are anything but scrupulously cleanly, and of which the sentiment of religious impurity, so intense in the Hindus, is a remarkable example. Suppose now that in a people of whom the majority were Mussulmans, that majority should insist upon not permitting pork to be eaten within the limits of the country. This would be nothing new in Mohammedan countries.* Would it be a legitimate exercise of the moral authority of public opinion, and if not, why not? The practice is really revolting to such a public. They also sincerely think that it is forbidden and abhorred by the Deity. Neither could the prohibition be censured as religious persecution. It might be religious in its origin, but it would not be persecution for religion, since nobody's religion makes it a duty to eat pork. The only tenable ground of condemnation would be that with the personal tastes and self-regarding concerns of individuals the public has no business to inferfere.

To come somewhat nearer home: the majority of Spaniards consider it a gross impiety, offensive in the highest degree to the Supreme Being, to worship him in any other manner than the Roman Catholic; and no other public worship is lawful on Spanish soil. The people of all southern Europe

* The case of the Bombay Parsees is a curious instance in point. When this industrious and enterprising tribe, the descendants of the Persian fire-worshipers, flying from their native country before the Caliphs, arrived in western India, they were admitted to toleration by the Hindu sovereigns, on condition of not eating beef. When those regions afterward fell under the dominion of Mohammedan conquerors, the Parsees obtained from them a continuance of indulgence, on condition of refraining from pork. What was at first obedience to authority became a second nature, and the Parsees to this day abstain both from beef and pork. Though not required by their religion, the double abstinence has had time to grow into a custom of their tribe; and custom, in the East, is a religion.

look upon a married clergy as not only irreligious, but unchaste, indecent, gross, disgusting. What do Protestants think of these perfectly sincere feelings, and of the attempt to enforce them against non-Catholics? Yet, if mankind are justified in interfering with each other's liberty in things which do not concern the interests of others, on what principle is it possible consistently to exclude these cases? Or who can blame people for desiring to suppress what they regard as a scandal in the sight of God and man? No stronger case can be shown for prohibiting anything which is regarded as a personal immorality than is made out for suppressing these practices in the eyes of those who regard them as impieties; and unless we are willing to adopt the logic of persecutors, and to say that we may persecute others because we are right, and that they must not persecute us because they are wrong, we must beware of admitting a principle of which we should resent as a gross injustice the application to ourselves.

The preceding instances may be objected to, although unreasonably, as drawn from contingencies impossible among us – opinion, in this country, not being likely to enforce abstinence from meats or to interfere with people for worshipping and for either marrying or not marrying, according to their creed or inclination. The next example, however, shall be taken from an interference with liberty which we have by no means passed all danger of. Wherever the Puritans have been sufficiently powerful, as in New England, and in Great Britain at the time of the Commonwealth, they have endeavoured, with considerable success, to put down all public, and nearly all private, amusements: especially music, dancing, public games, or other assemblages for purposes of diversion, and the theatre. There are still in this country large bodies of persons by whose notions of morality and religion these recreations are condemned; and those persons belonging chiefly to the middle class, who are the ascendant power in the present social and political condition of the kingdom, it is by no means impossible that persons of these sentiments may at some time or other command a majority in Parliament. How will the remaining portion of the community like to have the amusements that shall be permitted to them regulated by the religious and moral sentiments of the stricter Calvinists and Methodists? Would they not, with considerable peremptoriness, desire these intrusively pious members of society to mind their own business? This is precisely what should be said to every government and every public who have the pretension that no person shall enjoy any pleasure which they think wrong. But if the principle of the pretension be admitted, no one can reasonably object to its being acted on in the sense of the majority, or other preponderating power in the country; and all persons must be ready to conform to the idea of a Christian commonwealth as understood by the early settlers in New England, if a religious profession similar to theirs should ever succeed in regaining its lost ground, as religions supposed to be declining have so often been known to do.

To imagine another contingency, perhaps more likely to be realized than the one last mentioned. There is confessedly a strong tendency in the modern world towards a democratic constitution of society, accompanied or not by popular political institutions. It is affirmed that in the country where this tendency is most completely realized – where both society and the government are most democratic, the United States – the feeling of the majority, to whom any appearance of a more showy or costly style of living than they can hope to rival is disagreeable, operates as a tolerably effectual sumptuary law, and that in many parts of the Union it is really difficult for a person possessing a very large income to find any mode of spending it which will not incur popular disapprobation. Though such statements as these are doubtless much exaggerated as a representation of existing facts, the state of things they describe is not only a conceivable and possible, but a probable result of democratic feeling combined with the notion that the public has a right to a veto on the manner in which individuals shall spend their incomes. We have only further to suppose a considerable diffusion of Socialist opinions, and it may become infamous in the eyes of the majority to possess more property than some very small amount, or any income not earned by manual labour. Opinions similar in principle to these already prevail widely among the artisan class and weigh oppressively on those who are amenable to the opinion chiefly of that class, namely, its own members. It is known that the bad workmen who form the majority of the operatives in many branches of industry are decidedly of opinion that bad workmen ought to receive the same wages as good, and that no one ought to be allowed, through piecework or otherwise, to earn by superior skill or industry more than others can without it. And they employ a moral police, which occasionally becomes a physical one, to deter skilful workmen from receiving, and employers from giving, a larger remuneration for a more useful service. If the public have any jurisdiction over private concerns, I cannot see that these people are in fault, or that any individual's particular public can be blamed for asserting the same authority over his individual conduct which the general public asserts over people in general.

But, without dwelling upon supposititious cases, there are, in our own day, gross usurpations upon the liberty of private life actually practised, and still greater ones threatened with some expectation of success, and opinions propounded which assert an unlimited right in the public not only to prohibit by law everything which it thinks wrong, but, in order to get at what it thinks wrong, to prohibit a number of things which it admits to be innocent.

Under the name of preventing intemperance, the people of one English colony, and of nearly half the United States, have been interdicted by law from making any use whatever of fermented drinks, except for medical purposes, for prohibition of their sale is in fact, as it is intended to be, prohibition of their use.[27] And though the impracticability of executing the law has caused its repeal in several of the States which had adopted it, including the one from which it derives its name, an attempt has notwithstanding been commenced, and is prosecuted with considerable zeal by many of the professed philanthropists, to agitate for a similar law

27. The law prohibiting the sale of liquor was first enacted in the state of Maine in 1851 – hence known as the 'Maine Law'.

in this country. The association, or 'Alliance', as it terms itself, which has been formed for this purpose, has acquired some notoriety through the publicity given to a correspondence between its secretary and one of the very few English public men who hold that a politician's opinion ought to be founded on principles.[28] Lord Stanley's share in this correspondence is calculated to strengthen the hopes already built on him by those who know how rare such qualities as are manifested in some of his public appearances unhappily are among those who figure in political life. The organ of the Alliance, who would 'deeply deplore the recognition of any principle which could be wrested to justify bigotry and persecution', undertakes to point out the 'broad and impassable barrier' which divides such principles from those of the association. 'All matters relating to thought, opinion, conscience, appear to me,' he says, 'to be without the sphere of legislation; all pertaining to social act, habit, relation, subject only to a discretionary power vested in the State itself, and not in the individual, to be within it.' No mention is made of a third class, different from either of these, viz., acts and habits which are not social, but individual; although it is to this class, surely, that the act of drinking fermented liquors belongs. Selling fermented liquors, however, is trading, and trading is a social act. But the infringement complained of is not on the liberty of the seller, but on that of the buyer and consumer; since the State might just as well forbid him to drink wine as purposely make it impossible for him to obtain it. The secretary, however, says, 'I claim, as a citizen, a right to legislate whenever my social rights are invaded by the social act of another.' And now for the definition of these 'social rights': 'If anything invades my social rights, certainly the traffic in strong drink does. It destroys my primary right of

28. The United Kingdom Alliance was founded in 1852. In 1856 *The Times* published an exchange of letters between Samuel Pope, the secretary of the Alliance, and Lord Stanley (later Lord Derby, the 15th Earl). Mill's tribute to Stanley is all the more interesting because Stanley was a Conservative; his father, the Earl of Derby, was then leader of the Conservative Party.

security by constantly creating and stimulating social disorder. It invades my right of equality by deriving a profit from the creation of a misery I am taxed to support. It impedes my right to free moral and intellectual development by surrounding my path with dangers and by weakening and demoralizing society, from which I have a right to claim mutual aid and intercourse.' A theory of 'social rights' the like of which probably never before found its way into distinct language: being nothing short of this – that it is the absolute social right of every individual that every other individual shall act in every respect exactly as he ought; that whosoever fails thereof in the smallest particular violates my social right and entitles me to demand from the legislature the removal of the grievance. So monstrous a principle is far more dangerous than any single interference with liberty; there is no violation of liberty which it would not justify; it acknowledges no right to any freedom whatever, except perhaps to that of holding opinions in secret, without ever disclosing them; for the moment an opinion which I consider noxious passes anyone's lips, it invades all the 'social rights' attributed to me by the Alliance. The doctrine ascribes to all mankind a vested interest in each other's moral, intellectual, and even physical perfection, to be defined by each claimant according to his own standard.

Another important example of illegitimate interference with the rightful liberty of the individual, not simply threatened, but long since carried into triumphant effect, is Sabbatarian legislation. Without doubt, abstinence on one day in the week, so far as the exigencies of life permit, from the usual daily occupation, though in no respect religiously binding on any except Jews, is a highly beneficial custom. And inasmuch as this custom cannot be observed without a general consent to that effect among the industrious classes, therefore, in so far as some persons by working may impose the same necessity on others, it may be allowable and right that the law should guarantee to each the observance by others of the custom, by suspending the greater operations of industry on a particular day. But this justification, grounded on the direct interest which others have in each individual's observance of the practice, does not apply to the self-chosen occupations in which a person may think fit to employ his leisure, nor does it hold good, in the smallest degree, for legal restrictions on amusements. It is true that the amusement of some is the day's work of others; but the pleasure, not to say the useful recreation, of many is worth the labour of a few, provided the occupation is freely chosen and can be freely resigned. The operatives are perfectly right in thinking that if all worked on Sunday, seven days' work would have to be given for six days' wages; but so long as the great mass of employments are suspended, the small number who for the enjoyment of others must still work obtain a proportional increase of earnings; and they are not obliged to follow those occupations if they prefer leisure to emolument. If a further remedy is sought, it might be found in the establishment by custom of a holiday on some other day of the week for those particular classes of persons. The only ground, therefore, on which restrictions on Sunday amusements can be defended must be that they are religiously wrong – a motive of legislation which can never be too earnestly protested against. '*Deorum injuriae Diis curae.*' [29] It remains to be proved that society or any of its officers holds a commission from on high to avenge any supposed offence to Omnipotence which is not also a wrong to our fellow creatures. The notion that it is one man's duty that another should be religious was the foundation of all the religious persecutions ever perpetrated, and, if admitted, would fully justify them. Though the feeling which breaks out in the repeated attempts to stop railway travelling on Sunday, in the resistance to the opening of museums, and the like, has not the cruelty of the old persecutors, the state of mind indicated by it is fundamentally the same. It is a determination not to tolerate others in doing what is permitted by their religion, because it is not permitted by the persecutor's religion. It is a belief that God not only abominates the act of the misbeliever, but will not hold us guiltless if we leave him unmolested.

29. Offences to the gods are the concern of the gods.

I cannot refrain from adding to these examples of the little account commonly made of human liberty the language of downright persecution which breaks out from the press of this country whenever it feels called on to notice the remarkable phenomenon of Mormonism. Much might be said on the unexpected and instructive fact that an alleged new revelation and a religion founded on it – the product of palpable imposture, not even supported by the *prestige* of extraordinary qualities in its founder – is believed by hundreds of thousands, and has been made the foundation of a society in the age of newspapers, railways, and the electric telegraph. What here concerns us is that this religion, like other and better religions, has its martyrs: that its prophet and founder was, for his teaching, put to death by a mob; that others of its adherents lost their lives by the same lawless violence; that they were forcibly expelled, in a body, from the country in which they first grew up, while, now that they have been chased into a solitary recess in the midst of a desert, many in this country openly declare that it would be right (only that it is not convenient) to send an expedition against them and compel them by force to conform to the opinions of other people. The article of the Mormonite doctrine which is the chief provocative to the antipathy which thus breaks through the ordinary restraints of religious tolerance is its sanction of polygamy; which, though permitted to Mohammedans, and Hindus, and Chinese, seems to excite unquenchable animosity when practised by persons who speak English and profess to be a kind of Christians. No one has a deeper disapprobation than I have of this Mormon institution; both for other reasons and because, far from being in any way countenanced by the principle of liberty, it is a direct infraction of that principle, being a mere riveting of the chains of one half of the community, and an emancipation of the other from reciprocity of obligation towards them. Still, it must be remembered that this relation is as much voluntary on the part of the women concerned in it, and who may be deemed the sufferers by it, as is the case with any other form of the marriage institution; and however surprising this fact may appear, it has its explanation in the common ideas and customs of the world, which, teaching women to think marriage the one thing needful, make it intelligible that many a woman should prefer being one of several wives to not being a wife at all. Other countries are not asked to recognize such unions, or release any portion of their inhabitants from their own laws on the score of Mormonite opinions. But when the dissentients have conceded to the hostile sentiments of others far more than could justly be demanded; when they have left the countries to which their doctrines were unacceptable and established themselves in a remote corner of the earth, which they have been the first to render habitable to human beings, it is difficult to see on what principles but those of tyranny they can be prevented from living there under what laws they please, provided they commit no aggression on other nations and allow perfect freedom of departure to those who are dissatisfied with their ways. A recent writer, in some respects of considerable merit, proposes (to use his own words) not a crusade, but a *civilizade*, against this polygamous community, to put an end to what seems to him a retrograde step in civilization. It also appears so to me, but I am not aware that any community has a right to force another to be civilized. So long as the sufferers by the bad law do not invoke assistance from other communities, I cannot admit that persons entirely unconnected with them ought to step in and require that a condition of things with which all who are directly interested appear to be satisfied should be put an end to because it is a scandal to persons some thousands of miles distant who have no part or concern in it. Let them send missionaries, if they please, to preach against it; and let them, by any fair means (of which silencing the teachers is not one), oppose the progress of similar doctrines among their own people. If civilization has got the better of barbarism when barbarism had the world to itself, it is too much to profess to be afraid lest barbarism, after having been fairly got under, should revive and conquer civilization. A civilization that can thus succumb to its vanquished enemy must first have become so degenerate that neither its appointed priests and teachers, nor anybody else, has the capacity, or will take the trouble, to stand up for it. If this be so, the sooner such a civilization receives notice to quit, the better. It can only go on from bad to worse until destroyed and regenerated (like the Western Empire) by energetic barbarians.

CHAPTER V

Applications

THE principles asserted in these pages must be more generally admitted as the basis for discussion of details before a consistent application of them to all the various departments of government and morals can be attempted with any prospect of advantage. The few observations I propose to make on questions of detail are designed to illustrate the principles rather than to follow them out to their consequences. I offer not so much applications as specimens of application, which may serve to bring into greater clearness the meaning and limits of the two maxims which together form the entire doctrine of this essay, and to assist the judgement in holding the balance between them in the cases where it appears doubtful which of them is applicable to the case.

The maxims are, first, that the individual is not accountable to society for his actions in so far as these concern the interests of no person but himself. Advice, instruction, persuasion, and avoidance by other people, if thought necessary by them for their own good, are the only measures by which society can justifiably express its dislike or disapprobation of his conduct. Secondly, that for such actions as are prejudicial to the interests of others, the individual is accountable and may be subjected either to social or to legal punishment if society is of opinion that the one or the other is requisite for its protection.

In the first place, it must by no means be supposed, because damage, or probability of damage, to the interests of others, can alone justify the interference of society, that therefore it always does justify such interference. In many cases an individual, in pursuing a legitimate object, necessarily and therefore legitimately causes pain or loss to others, or intercepts a good which they had a reasonable hope of obtaining. Such oppositions of interest between individuals often arise from bad social institutions, but are unavoidable while those institutions last;

and some would be unavoidable under any institutions. Whoever succeeds in an overcrowded profession or in a competitive examination, whoever is preferred to another in any contest for an object which both desire, reaps benefit from the loss of others, from their wasted exertion and their disappointment. But it is, by common admission, better for the general interest of mankind that persons should pursue their objects undeterred by this sort of consequences. In other words, society admits no right, either legal or moral, in the disappointed competitors to immunity from this kind of suffering, and feels called on to interfere only when means of success have been employed which it is contrary to the general interest to permit – namely, fraud or treachery, and force.

Again, trade is a social act. Whoever undertakes to sell any description of goods to the public does what affects the interest of other persons, and of society in general; and thus his conduct, in principle, comes within the jurisdiction of society; accordingly, it was once held to be the duty of governments, in all cases which were considered of importance, to fix prices and regulate the processes of manufacture. But it is now recognized, though not till after a long struggle, that both the cheapness and the good quality of commodities are most effectually provided for by leaving the producers and sellers perfectly free, under the sole check of equal freedom to the buyers for supplying themselves elsewhere. This is the so-called doctrine of 'free trade', which rests on grounds different from, though equally solid with, the principle of individual liberty asserted in this essay. Restrictions on trade, or on production for purposes of trade, are indeed restraints; and all restraint, *qua* restraint, is an evil; but the restraints in question affect only that part of conduct which society is competent to restrain, and are wrong solely because they do not really produce the results which it is desired to produce by them. As the principle of individual liberty is not involved in the doctrine of free trade, so neither is it in most of the questions which arise respecting the limits of that doctrine, as, for example, what amount of public control is admissible for the prevention of fraud by adulteration;

how far sanitary precautions, or arrangements to protect workpeople employed in dangerous occupations, should be enforced on employers. Such questions involve considerations of liberty only in so far as leaving people to themselves is always better, *caeteris paribus*,[30] than controlling them; but that they may be legitimately controlled for these ends is in principle undeniable. On the other hand, there are questions relating to interference with trade which are essentially questions of liberty, such as the Maine Law, already touched upon;[31] the prohibition of the importation of opium into China; the restriction of the sale of poisons – all cases, in short, where the object of the interference is to make it impossible or difficult to obtain a particular commodity. These interferences are objectionable, not as infringements on the liberty of the producer or seller, but on that of the buyer.

One of these examples, that of the sale of poisons, opens a new question: the proper limits of what may be called the functions of police; how far liberty may legitimately be invaded for the prevention of crime, or of accident. It is one of the undisputed functions of government to take precautions against crime before it has been committed, as well as to detect and punish it afterwards. The preventive function of government, however, is far more liable to be abused, to the prejudice of liberty, than the punitory function; for there is hardly any part of the legitimate freedom of action of a human being which would not admit of being represented, and fairly, too, as increasing the facilities for some form or other of delinquency. Nevertheless, if a public authority, or even a private person, sees anyone evidently preparing to commit a crime, they are not bound to look on inactive until the crime is committed, but may interfere to prevent it. If poisons were never bought or used for any purpose except the commission of murder, it would be right to prohibit their manufacture and sale. They may, however, be wanted not only for innocent but for useful purposes, and restrictions cannot be imposed in the one case without operating in the other. Again, it is a

30. Other things being equal.
31. See above, p. 156.

proper office of public authority to guard against accidents. If either a public officer or anyone else saw a person attempting to cross a bridge which had been ascertained to be unsafe, and there were no time to warn him of his danger, they might seize him and turn him back, without any real infringement of his liberty; for liberty consists in doing what one desires, and he does not desire to fall into the river. Nevertheless, when there is not a certainty, but only a danger of mischief, no one but the person himself can judge of the sufficiency of the motive which may prompt him to incur the risk; in this case, therefore (unless he is a child, or delirious, or in some state of excitement or absorption incompatible with the full use of the reflecting faculty), he ought, I conceive, to be only warned of the danger; not forcibly prevented from exposing himself to it. Similar considerations, applied to such a question as the sale of poisons, may enable us to decide which among the possible modes of regulation are or are not contrary to principle. Such a precaution, for example, as that of labelling the drug with some word expressive of its dangerous character may be enforced without violation of liberty: the buyer cannot wish not to know that the thing he possesses has poisonous qualities. But to require in all cases the certificate of a medical practitioner would make it sometimes impossible, always expensive, to obtain the article for legitimate uses. The only mode apparent to me, in which difficulties may be thrown in the way of crime committed through this means, without any infringement worth taking into account upon the liberty of those who desire the poisonous substance for other purposes, consists in providing what, in the apt language of Bentham, is called 'preappointed evidence'.[32] This provision is familiar to everyone in the case of contracts. It is usual and right that the law, when a contract is entered into, should require as the condition of its enforcing performance that certain formalities should be observed, such as signatures, attestation of witnesses, and the like, in order that in case of

32. The term appears in Book IV of Bentham's *Rationale of Judicial Evidence*, a work edited by Mill in his youth. (Bentham, *Collected Works*, ed. John Bowring [London, 1843], vol. VI, pp. 508 ff.)

subsequent dispute there may be evidence to prove that the contract was really entered into, and that there was nothing in the circumstances to render it legally invalid, the effect being to throw great obstacles in the way of fictitious contracts, or contracts made in circumstances which, if known, would destroy their validity. Precautions of a similar nature might be enforced in the sale of articles adapted to be instruments of crime. The seller, for example, might be required to enter in a register the exact time of the transaction, the name and address of the buyer, the precise quality and quantity sold; to ask the purpose for which it was wanted, and record the answer he received. When there was no medical prescription, the presence of some third person might be required to bring home the fact to the purchaser, in case there should afterwards be reason to believe that the article had been applied to criminal purposes. Such regulations would in general be no material impediment to obtaining the article, but a very considerable one to making an improper use of it without detection.

The right inherent in society to ward off crimes against itself by antecedent precautions suggests the obvious limitations to the maxim that purely self-regarding misconduct cannot properly be meddled with in the way of prevention or punishment. Drunkenness, for example, in ordinary cases, is not a fit subject for legislative interference, but I should deem it perfectly legitimate that a person who had once been convicted of any act of violence to others under the influence of drink should be placed under a special legal restriction, personal to himself; that if he were afterwards found drunk, he should be liable to a penalty, and that if, when in that state, he committed another offence, the punishment to which he would be liable for that other offence should be increased in severity. The making himself drunk, in a person whom drunkenness excites to do harm to others, is a crime against others. So, again, idleness, except in a person receiving support from the public, or except when it constitutes a breach of contract, cannot without tyranny be made a subject of legal punishment; but if, either from idleness or from any other avoidable cause, a man fails to perform his legal duties to others, as for instance to support his children, it is no tyranny to force him to fulfil that obligation by compulsory labour if no other means are available.

Again, there are many acts which, being directly injurious only to the agents themselves, ought not to be legally interdicted, but which, if done publicly, are a violation of good manners and, coming thus within the category of offences against others, may rightly be prohibited. Of this kind are offences against decency; on which it is unnecessary to dwell, the rather as they are only connected indirectly with our subject, the objection to publicity being equally strong in the case of many actions not in themselves condemnable, nor supposed to be so.

There is another question to which an answer must be found, consistent with the principles which have been laid down. In cases of personal conduct supposed to be blameable, but which respect for liberty precludes society from preventing or punishing because the evil directly resulting falls wholly on the agent; what the agent is free to do, ought other persons to be equally free to counsel or instigate? This question is not free from difficulty. The case of a person who solicits another to do an act is not strictly a case of self-regarding conduct. To give advice or offer inducements to anyone is a social act and may, therefore, like actions in general which affect others, be supposed amenable to social control. But a little reflection corrects the first impression, by showing that if the case is not strictly within the definition of individual liberty, yet the reasons on which the principle of individual liberty is grounded are applicable to it. If people must be allowed, in whatever concerns only themselves, to act as seems best to themselves, at their own peril, they must equally be free to consult with one another about what is fit to be so done; to exchange opinions, and give and receive suggestions. Whatever it is permitted to do, it must be permitted to advise to do. The question is doubtful only when the instigator derives a personal benefit from his advice, when he makes it his occupation, for subsistence or pecuniary gain, to promote what society and the State consider to be an evil. Then, indeed, a new element of complication is introduced – namely, the existence of classes of persons with an interest opposed to what is considered as the public weal, and whose mode of living is grounded on the counteraction of it. Ought this to be interfered with, or not? Fornication, for example, must be tolerated, and so must gambling; but should a person be free to be a pimp, or to keep a gambling house? The case is one of those which lie on the exact boundary line between two principles, and it is not at once apparent to which of the two it properly belongs. There are arguments on both sides. On the side of toleration it may be said that the fact of following anything as an occupation, and living or profiting by the practice of it, cannot make that criminal which would otherwise be admissible; that the act should either be consistently permitted or consistently prohibited; that if the principles which we have hitherto defended are true, society has no business, *as* society, to decide anything to be wrong which concerns only the individual; that it cannot go beyond dissuasion, and that one person should be as free to persuade as another to dissuade. In opposition to this it may be contended that, although the public, or the State, are not warranted in authoritatively deciding, for purposes of repression or punishment, that such or such conduct affecting only the interests of the individual is good or bad, they are fully justified in assuming, if they regard it as bad, that its being so or not is at least a disputable question: that, this being supposed, they cannot be acting wrongly in endeavouring to exclude the influence of solicitations which are not disinterested, of instigators who cannot possibly be impartial – who have a direct personal interest on one side, and that side the one which the State believes to be wrong, and who confessedly promote it for personal objects only. There can surely, it may be urged, be nothing lost, no sacrifice of good, by so ordering matters that persons shall make their election, either wisely or foolishly, on their own prompting, as free as possible from the arts of persons who stimulate their inclinations for interested purposes of their own. Thus (it may be said), though the statutes respecting unlawful games are utterly indefensible – though all persons should be free to gamble in their own or each other's houses, or in any place of meeting established by their own subscriptions and open only to the members and their visitors – yet public gambling houses should not be permitted. It is true that the prohibition is never effectual, and that, whatever amount of tyrannical power may be given to the police, gambling houses can always be maintained under other pretences; but they may be compelled to conduct their operations with a certain degree of secrecy and mystery, so that nobody knows anything about them but those who seek them; and more than this society ought not to aim at. There is considerable force in these arguments. I will not venture to decide whether they are sufficient to justify the moral anomaly of punishing the accessory when the principal is (and must be) allowed to go free; of fining or imprisoning the procurer, but not the fornicator – the gambling-house keeper, but not the gambler. Still less ought the common operations of buying and selling to be interfered with on analogous grounds. Almost every article which is bought and sold may be used in excess, and the sellers have a pecuniary interest in encouraging that excess; but no argument can be founded on this in favour, for instance, of the Maine Law; because the class of dealers in strong drinks, though interested in their abuse, are indispensably required for the sake of their legitimate use. The interest, however, of these dealers in promoting intemperance is a real evil and justifies the State in imposing restrictions and requiring guarantees which, but for that justification, would be infringements of legitimate liberty.

A further question is whether the State, while it permits, should nevertheless indirectly discourage conduct which it deems contrary to the best interests of the agent; whether, for example, it should take measures to render the means of drunkenness more costly, or add to the difficulty of procuring them by limiting the number of the places of sale. On this, as on most other practical questions, many distinctions require to be made. To tax stimulants for the sole purpose of making them more difficult to be obtained is a measure differing only in degree from their entire prohibition, and would be justifiable only if that were justifiable. Every increase of cost is a prohibition to those whose means do not come up to the augmented price; and to those who do, it is a penalty laid on them for gratifying a particular taste. Their choice of pleasures and their mode of expending their income, after satisfying their legal and moral obligations to the State and to individuals, are their own concern and must rest with their own judgement. These considerations may seem at first sight to condemn the selection of stimulants as special subjects of taxation for purposes of revenue. But it must be remembered that taxation for fiscal purposes is absolutely inevitable; that in most countries it is necessary that a considerable part of that taxation should be indirect; that the State, therefore, cannot help imposing penalties, which to some persons may be prohibitory, on the use of some articles of consumption. It is hence the duty of the State to consider, in the imposition of taxes, what commodities the consumers can best spare; and *a fortiori*, to select in preference those of which it deems the use, beyond a very moderate quantity, to be positively injurious. Taxation, therefore, of stimulants up to the point which produces the largest amount of revenue (supposing that the State needs all the revenue which it yields) is not only admissible, but to be approved of.

The question of making the sale of these commodities a more or less exclusive privilege must be answered differently, according to the purposes to which the restriction is intended to be subservient. All places of public resort require the restraint of a police, and places of this kind peculiarly, because offences against society are especialy apt to originate there. It is, therefore, fit to confine the power of selling these commodities (at least for consumption on the spot) to persons of known or vouched-for respectability of conduct; to make such regulations respecting hours of opening and closing as may be requisite for public surveillance, and to withdraw the licence if breaches of the peace repeatedly take place through the connivance or incapacity of the keeper of the house, or if it becomes a rendezvous for concocting and preparing offences against the law. Any further restriction I do not conceive to be, in principle, justifiable. The limitation in number, for instance, of beer and spirit houses, for the express purpose of rendering them more difficult of access and diminishing the occasions of temptation, not only exposes all to an inconvenience because there are some by whom the facility would be abused, but is suited only to a state of society in which the labouring classes are avowedly treated as children or savages, and placed under an education of restraint, to fit them for future admission to the privileges of freedom. This is not the principle on which the labouring classes are professedly governed in any free country; and no person who sets due value on freedom will give his adhesion to their being so governed, unless after all efforts have been exhausted to educate them for freedom and govern them as freemen, and it has been definitely proved that they can only be governed as children. The bare statement of the alternative shows the absurdity of supposing that such efforts have been made in any case which needs be considered here. It is only because the institutions of this country are a mass of inconsistencies, that things find admittance into our practice which belong to the system of despotic, or what is called paternal, government, while the general freedom of our institutions precludes the exercise of the amount of control necessary to render the restraint of any real efficacy as a moral education.

It was pointed out in an early part of this essay that the liberty of the individual, in things wherein the individual is alone concerned, implies a corresponding liberty in any number of individuals to regulate by mutual agreement such things as regard them jointly, and regard no persons but themselves. This question presents no difficulty so long as the will of all the persons implicated remains unaltered; but since that will may change, it is often necessary, even in things in which they alone are concerned, that they should enter into engagements with one another; and when they do, it is fit, as a general rule, that those engagements should be kept. Yet, in the laws, probably, of every country, this general rule has some exceptions. Not only persons are not held to engagements which violate the rights of third parties, but it is sometimes considered a sufficient reason for releasing them from an engagement that it is injurious to themselves. In this and most other civilized countries, for example, an engagement by which a person should sell himself, or allow himself to be sold, as a slave would be null and void, neither enforced by law nor by opinion. The ground for thus limiting his power of voluntarily disposing of his own lot in life is apparent, and is very clearly seen in this extreme case. The reason for not interfering, unless for the sake of others, with a person's voluntary acts is consideration for his liberty. His voluntary choice is evidence that what he so chooses is desirable, or at least endurable, to him, and his good is on the whole best provided for by allowing him to take his own means of pursuing it. But by selling himself for a slave, he abdicates his liberty; he foregoes any future use of it beyond that single act. He therefore defeats, in his own case, the very purpose which is the justification of allowing him to dispose of himself. He is no longer free, but is thenceforth in a position which has no longer the presumption in its favour that would be afforded by his voluntarily remaining in it. The principle of freedom cannot require that he should be free not to be free. It is not freedom to be allowed to alienate his freedom. These reasons, the force of which is so conspicuous in this peculiar case, are evidently of far wider application, yet a limit is everywhere set to them by the necessities of life, which continually require, not indeed that we should resign our freedom, but that we should consent to this and the other limitation of it. The principle, however, which demands uncontrolled freedom of action in all that concerns only the agents themselves, requires that those who have become bound to one another, in things which concern no third party, should be able to release one another from the engagement; and even without such voluntary release there are perhaps no contracts or engagements, except those that relate to money or money's worth, of which one can venture to say that there ought to be no liberty whatever of retraction. Baron Wilhelm von Humboldt, in the excellent essay from which I have already quoted, states it as his conviction that engagements which involve personal relations or services should never be legally binding beyond a limited duration of time; and that the most important of these engagements, marriage, having the peculiarity that its objects are frustrated unless the feelings of both the parties are in harmony with it, should require nothing more than the declared will of either party to dissolve it. This subject is too important and too complicated to be discussed in a parenthesis, and I touch on it only so far as is necessary for purposes of illustration. If the conciseness and generality of Baron Humboldt's dissertation had not obliged him in this instance to content himself with enunciating his conclusion without discussing the premises, he would doubtless have recognized that the question cannot be decided on grounds so simple as those to which he confines himself. When a person, either by express promise or by conduct, has encouraged another to rely on his continuing to act in a certain way – to build expectations and calculations, and stake any part of his plan of life upon that supposition – a new series of moral obligations arises on his part towards that person, which may possibly be overruled, but cannot be ignored. And again, if the relation between two contracting parties has been followed by consequences to others; if it has placed third parties in any peculiar position, or, as in the case of marriage, has even called third parties into existence, obligations arise on the part of both the contracting parties towards those third persons, the fulfilment of which, or at all events the mode of fulfilment, must be greatly affected by the continuance or disruption of the relation between the original parties to the contract. It does not follow, nor can I admit, that these obligations extend to requiring the fulfilment of the contract at all costs to the happiness of the reluctant party; but they are a necessary element in the question; and even if, as von Humboldt maintains, they ought to make no difference in the *legal* freedom of the parties to release themselves from the engagement (and I also hold that they ought not to make *much* difference), they necessarily make a great difference in the *moral* freedom. A person is bound to take all these circumstances into account before resolving on a step which may affect such important interests of others; and if he does not allow proper weight to those interests, he is morally responsible for the wrong. I have made these obvious remarks for the better illustration of the general principle of liberty, and not because they are at all needed on the particular question, which, on the contrary, is usually discussed as if the interest of children was everything, and that of grown persons nothing.

I have already observed that, owing to the absence of any recognized general principles, liberty is often granted where it should be withheld, as well as withheld where it should be granted; and one of the cases in which, in the modern European world, the sentiment of liberty is the strongest is a case where, in my view, it is altogether misplaced. A person should be free to do as he likes in his own concerns, but he ought not to be free to do as he likes in acting for another, under the pretext that the affairs of the other are his own affairs. The State, while it respects the liberty of each in what specially regards himself, is bound to maintain a vigilant control over his exercise of any power which it allows him to possess over others. This obligation is almost entirely disregarded in the case of the family relations – a case, in its direct influence on human happiness, more important than all others taken together. The almost despotic power of husbands over wives needs not be enlarged upon here, because nothing more is needed for the complete removal of the evil than that wives should have the same rights and should receive the protection of law in the same manner as all other persons; and because, on this subject, the defenders of established injustice do not avail themselves of the plea of liberty but stand forth openly as the champions of power. It is in the case of children that misapplied notions of liberty are a real obstacle to the fulfilment by the State of its duties. One would almost think that a man's children were supposed to be literally, and not metaphorically, a part of himself, so jealous is opinion of the smallest interference of law with his absolute and exclusive control over them, more jealous than of almost any interference with his own freedom of action: so much less do the generality of mankind value liberty than power. Consider, for example, the case of education. Is it not almost a self-evident axiom that the State should require and compel the education, up to a certain standard, of every human being who is born its citizen? Yet who is there that is not afraid to recognize and assert this truth? Hardly anyone, indeed, will deny that it is one of the most sacred duties of the parents (or, as law and usage now stand, the father), after summoning a human being into the world, to give to that being an education fitting him to perform his part well in life towards others and towards himself. But while this is unanimously declared to be the father's duty, scarcely anybody, in this country, will bear to hear of obliging him to perform it. Instead of his being required to make any exertion or sacrifice for securing education to his child, it is left to his choice to accept it or not when it is provided gratis! It still remains unrecognized that to bring a child into existence without a fair prospect of being able, not only to provide food for its body, but instruction and training for its mind is a moral crime, both against the unfortunate offspring and against society; and that if the parent does not fulfil this obligation, the State ought to see it fulfilled at the charge, as far as possible, of the parent.

Were the duty of enforcing universal education once admitted there would be an end to the difficulties about what the State should teach, and how it should teach, which now convert the subject into a mere battlefield for sects and parties, causing the time and labour which should have been spent in educating to be wasted in quarrelling about education. If the government would make up its mind to require for every child a good education, it might save itself the trouble of providing one. It might leave to parents to obtain the education where and how they pleased, and content itself with helping to pay the school fees of the poorer classes of children, and defraying the entire school expenses of those who have no one else to pay for them. The objections which are urged with reason against State education do not apply to the enforcement of education by the State, but to the State's taking upon itself to direct that education; which is a totally different thing. That the whole or any large part of the education of the people should be in State hands, I go as far as anyone in deprecating. All that has been said of the importance of individuality of character, and diversity in opinions and modes of conduct, involves, as of the same unspeakable importance, diversity of education. A general State education is a mere contrivance for moulding people to be exactly like one another; and as the mould in which it casts them is that which pleases the predominant power in the government – whether this be a monarch, a priesthood, an aristocracy, or the majority of the existing generation – in proportion as it is efficient and successful, it establishes a despotism over the mind, leading by natural tendency to one over the body. An education established and controlled by the State should only exist, if it exist at all, as one among many competing experiments, carried on for the purpose of example and stimulus to keep the others up to a certain standard of excellence. Unless, indeed, when society in general is in so backward a state that it could not or would not provide for itself any proper institutions of education unless the government undertook the task, then, indeed, the government may, as the less of two great evils, take upon itself the business of schools and universities, as it may that of joint stock companies when private enterprise in a shape fitted for undertaking great works of industry does not exist in the country. But in general, if the country contains a sufficient number of persons qualified to provide education under government auspices, the same persons would be able and willing to give an equally good education on the voluntary principle, under the assurance of remuneration afforded by a law rendering education compulsory, combined with State aid to those unable to defray the expense.

The instrument for enforcing the law could be no other than public examinations, extending to all children and beginning at an early age. An age might be fixed at which every child must be examined, to ascertain if he (or she) is able to read. If a child proves unable, the father, unless he has some sufficient ground of excuse, might be subjected to a moderate fine, to be worked out, if necessary, by his labour, and the child might be put to school at his expense. Once in every year the examination should be renewed, with a gradually extending range of subjects, so as to make the universal acquisition and, what is more, retention of a certain minimum of general knowledge virtually compulsory. Beyond that minimum there should be voluntary examinations on all subjects, at which all who come up to a certain standard of proficiency might claim a certificate. To prevent the State from exercising, through these arrangements, an improper influence over opinion, the knowledge required for passing an examination (beyond the merely instrumental parts of knowledge, such as languages and their use) should, even in the higher classes of examinations, be confined to facts and positive science exclusively. The examinations on religion, politics, or other disputed topics should not turn on the truth or falsehood of opinions, but on the matter of fact that such and such an opinion is held, on such grounds, by such authors, or schools, or churches. Under this system, the rising generation would be no worse off in regard to all disputed truths than they are at present; they would be brought up either churchmen or dissenters as they now are, the State merely taking care that they should be instructed churchmen, or instructed dissenters. There would be nothing to hinder them from being taught religion, if their parents chose, at the same schools where they were taught other things. All attempts by the State to bias the conclusions of its citizens on disputed subjects are evil; but it may very properly offer to ascertain and certify that a person possesses the knowledge requisite to make his conclusions on any given subject worth attending to. A student of philosophy would be the better for being able to stand an examination both in Locke and in Kant, whichever of the two he takes up with, or even if with neither: and there is no reasonable objection to examining an atheist in the evidences of Christianity, provided he is not required to profess a belief in them. The examinations, however, in the higher branches of knowledge should, I conceive, be entirely voluntary. It would be giving too dangerous a power to governments were they allowed to exclude anyone from professions, even from the profession of teacher, for alleged deficiency of qualifications; and I think, with Wilhelm von Humboldt, that degrees or other public certificates of scientific or professional acquirements should be given to all who present themselves for examination and stand the test, but that such certificates should confer no advantage over competitors other than the weight which may be attached to their testimony by public opinion.

It is not in the matter of education only that misplaced notions of liberty prevent moral obligations on the part of parents from being recognized, and legal obligations from being imposed, where there are the strongest grounds for the former always, and in many cases for the latter also. The fact itself, of causing the existence of a human being, is one of the most responsible actions in the range of human life. To undertake this responsibility – to bestow a life which may be either a curse or a blessing – unless the being on whom it is to be bestowed will have at least the ordinary chances of a desirable existence, is a crime against that being. And in a country, either overpeopled or threatened with being so, to produce children, beyond a very small number, with the effect of reducing the reward of labour by their competition is a serious offence against all who live by the remuneration of their labour. The laws which, in many countries on the Continent, forbid marriage unless the parties can show that they have the means of supporting a family do not exceed the legitimate powers of the State; and whether such laws be expedient or not (a question mainly dependent on local circumstances and feelings), they are not objectionable as violations of liberty. Such laws are interferences of the State to prohibit a mischievous act – an act injurious to others, which ought to be a subject of reprobation and social stigma, even when it is not deemed expedient to superadd legal punishment. Yet the current ideas of liberty, which bend so easily to real infringements of the freedom of the individual in things which concern only himself, would repel the attempt to put any restraint upon his inclinations when the consequence of their indulgence is a life or lives of wretchedness and depravity to the offspring, with manifold evils to those sufficiently within reach to be in any way affected by their actions. When we compare the strange respect of mankind for liberty with their strange want of respect for it, we might imagine that a man had an indispensable right to do harm to others, and no right at all to please himself without giving pain to anyone.

I have reserved for the last place a large class of questions respecting the limits of government interference, which, though closely connected with the subject of this essay, do not, in strictness, belong to it. These are cases in which the reasons against interference do not turn upon the principle of liberty: the question is not about restraining the actions of individuals, but about helping them; it is asked whether the government should do, or cause to be done, something for their benefit instead of leaving it to be done by themselves, individually or in voluntary combination.

The objections to government interference, when it is not such as to involve infringement of liberty, may be of three kinds:

The first is when the thing to be done is likely to be better done by individuals than by the government. Speaking generally, there is no one so fit to conduct any business, or to determine how or by whom it shall be conducted, as those who are personally interested in it. This principle condemns the interferences, once so common, of the legislature, or the officers of government, with the ordinary processes of industry. But this part of the subject has been sufficiently enlarged upon by political economists, and is not particularly related to the principles of this essay.

The second objection is more nearly allied to our subject. In many cases, though individuals may not do the particular thing so well, on the average, as the officers of government, it is nevertheless desirable that it should be done by them, rather than by the government, as a means to their own mental education – a mode of strengthening their active faculties, exercising their judgement, and giving them a familiar knowledge of the subjects with which they are thus left to deal. This is a principal, though not the sole, recommendation of jury trial (in cases not political); of free and popular local and municipal institutions; of the conduct of industrial and philanthropic enterprises by voluntary associations. These are not questions of liberty, and are connected with that subject only by remote tendencies, but they are questions of development. It belongs to a different occasion from the present to dwell on these things as parts of national education, as being, in truth, the peculiar training of a citizen, the practical part of the political education of a free people, taking them out of the narrow circle of personal and family selfishness, and accustoming them to the comprehension of joint interests, the management of joint concerns – habituating them to act from public or semi-public motives, and guide their conduct by aims which unite instead of isolating them from one another. Without these habits and powers, a free constitution can neither be worked nor preserved, as is exemplified by the too-often transitory nature of political freedom in countries where it does not rest upon a sufficient basis of local liberties. The management of purely local business by the localities, and of the great enterprises of industry by the union of those who voluntarily supply the pecuniary means, is further recommended by all the advantages which have been set forth in this essay as belonging to individuality of development and diversity of modes of action. Government operations tend to be everywhere alike. With individuals and voluntary associations, on the contrary, there are varied experiments and endless diversity of experience. What the State can usefully do is to make itself a central depository, and active circulator and diffuser, of the experience resulting from many trials. Its business is to enable each experimentalist to benefit by the experiments of others, instead of tolerating no experiments but its own.

The third and most cogent reason for restricting the interference of government is the great evil of adding unnecessarily to its power. Every function superadded to those already exercised by the government causes its influence over hopes and fears to be more widely diffused, and converts, more and more, the active and ambitious part of the public into hangers-on of the government, or of some party which aims at becoming the government. If the roads, the railways, the banks, the insurance offices, the great joint-stock companies, the universities, and the public charities were all of them branches of the government; if, in addition, the municipal corporations and local boards, with all that now devolves on them, became departments of the central administration; if the employees of all these different enterprises were appointed and paid by the government and looked to the government for every rise in life, not all the freedom of the press and popular constitution of the legislature would make this or any other country free otherwise than in name. And the evil would be greater, the more efficiently and scientifically the administrative machinery was constructed – the more skilful the arrangements for obtaining the best qualified hands and heads with which to work it. In England it has of late been proposed that all the members of the civil service of government should be selected by competitive examination, to obtain for these employments the most intelligent and instructed persons procurable; and much has been said and written for and against this proposal. One of the arguments most insisted on by its opponents is that the occupation of a permanent official servant of the State does not hold out sufficient prospects of emolument and importance to attract the highest talents, which will always be able to find a more inviting career in the professions or in the service of companies and other public bodies. One would not have been surprised if this argument had been used by the friends of the proposition as an answer to its principal difficulty. Coming from the opponents it is strange enough. What is urged as an objection is the safety valve of the proposed system. If, indeed, all the high talent of the country *could* be drawn into the service of the government, a proposal tending to bring about that result might well inspire uneasiness. If every part of the business of society which required organized concert, or large and comprehensive views, were in the hands of the government, and if government offices were universally filled by the ablest men, all the enlarged culture and practised intelligence in the country, except the purely speculative, would be concentrated in a numerous bureaucracy, to whom alone the rest of the community would look for all things – the multitude for direction and dictation in all they had to do; the able and aspiring for personal advancement. To be admitted into the ranks of this bureaucracy, and when admitted, to rise therein, would be the sole objects of ambition. Under this *régime* not only is the outside public ill-qualified, for want of practical experience, to criticize or check the mode of operation of the bureaucracy, but even if the accidents of despotic or the natural working of popular institutions occasionally raise to the summit a ruler or rulers of reforming inclinations, no reform can be effected which is contrary to the interest of the bureaucracy. Such is the melancholy condition of the Russian empire, as shown in the accounts of those who have had sufficient opportunity of observation. The Czar himself is powerless against the bureaucratic body: he can send any one of them to Siberia, but he cannot govern without them, or against their will. On every decree of his they have a tacit veto, by merely refraining from carrying it into effect. In countries of more advanced civilization and of a more insurrectionary spirit, the public, accustomed to expect everything to be done for them by the State, or at least to do nothing for themselves without asking from the State not only leave to do it, but even how it is to be done, naturally hold the State responsible for all evil which befalls them, and when the evil exceeds their amount of patience, they rise against the government and make what is called a revolution; whereupon somebody else, with or without legitimate authority from the nation, vaults into the seat, issues his orders to the bureaucracy, and everything goes on much as it did before; the bureaucracy being unchanged, and nobody else being capable of taking their place.

A very different spectacle is exhibited among a people accustomed to transact their own business. In France, a large part of the people, having been engaged in military service, many of whom have held at least the rank of non-commissioned officers, there are in every popular insurrection several persons competent to take the lead and improvise some tolerable plan of action. What the French are in military affairs, the Americans are in every kind of civil business; let them be left without a government, every body of Americans is able to improvise one and to carry on that or any other public business with a sufficient amount of intelligence, order, and decision. This is what every free people ought to be: and a people capable of this is certain to be free; it will never let itself be enslaved by any man or body of men because these are able to seize and pull the reins of the central administration. No bureaucracy can hope to make such a people as this do or undergo anything that they do not like. But where everything is done through the bureaucracy, nothing to which the bureaucracy is really adverse can be done at all. The constitution of such countries is an organization of the experience and practical ability of the nation into a disciplined body for the purpose of governing the rest; and the more perfect that organization is in itself, the more successful in drawing to itself and educating for itself the persons of greatest capacity from all ranks of the community, the more complete is the bondage of all, the members of the bureaucracy included. For the governors are as much the slaves of their organization and discipline as the governed are of the governors. A Chinese mandarin is as much the tool and creature of a despotism as the humblest cultivator. An individual Jesuit is to the utmost degree of abasement the slave of his order, though the order itself exists for the collective power and importance of its members.

It is not, also, to be forgotten that the absorption of all the principal ability of the country into the governing body is fatal, sooner or later, to the mental activity and progressiveness of the body itself. Banded together as they are – working a system which, like all systems, necessarily proceeds in a great measure by fixed rules – the official body are under the constant temptation of sinking into indolent routine, or, if they now and then desert that mill-horse round, of rushing into some half-examined crudity which has struck the fancy of some leading member of the corps; and the sole check to these closely allied, though seemingly opposite, tendencies, the only stimulus which can keep the ability of the body itself up to a high standard, is liability to the watchful criticism of equal ability outside the body. It is indispensable, therefore, that the means should exist, independently of the government, of forming such ability and furnishing it with the opportunities and experience necessary for a correct judgement of great practical affairs. If we would possess permanently a skilful and efficient body of functionaries – above all a body able to originate and willing to adopt improvements – if we would not have our bureaucracy degenerate into a pedanto-cracy, this body must not engross all the occupations which form and cultivate the faculties required for the government of mankind.

To determine the point at which evils, so formidable to human freedom and advancement, begin, or rather at which they begin to predominate over the benefits attending the collective application of the force of society, under its recog-nized chiefs, for the removal of the obstacles which stand in the way of its well-being; to secure as much of the advantages of centralized power and intelligence as can be had without turning into governmental channels too great a proportion of the general activity – is one of the most difficult and compli-cated questions in the art of government. It is, in a great measure, a question of detail in which many and various considerations must be kept in view, and no absolute rule can be laid down. But I believe that the practical principle in which safety resides, the ideal to be kept in view, the standard by which to test all arrangements intended for overcoming the difficulty, may be conveyed in these words: the greatest dissemination of power consistent with efficiency; but the greatest possible centralization of information and diffusion of it from the centre. Thus, in municipal administration, there would be, as in the New England states, a very minute division among separate officers, chosen by the localities, of all business which is not better left to the persons directly interested; but besides this, there would be, in each department of local affairs, a central superintendence, forming a branch of the general government. The organ of this superintendence would concentrate, as in a focus, the variety of information and experience derived from the conduct of that branch of public business in all the localities, from everything analogous which is done in foreign countries, and from the general principles of political science. This central organ should have a right to know all that is done, and its special duty should be that of making the knowledge acquired in one place available for others. Emancipated from the petty prejudices and narrow views of a locality by its elevated position and comprehensive sphere of observation, its advice would naturally carry much authority; but its actual power, as a permanent institution, should, I conceive, be limited to compelling the local officers to obey the laws laid down for their guidance. In all things not provided for by general rules, those officers should be left to their own judgement, under responsibility to their constituents. For the violation of rules, they should be responsible to law, and the rules themselves should be laid down by the legislature; the central administrative authority only watching over their execution and, if they were not properly carried into effect, appealing, according to the nature of the case, to the tribunals to enforce the law, or to the constituencies to dismiss the functionaries who had not executed it according to its spirit. Such, in its general conception, is the central superintendence which the Poor Law Board is intended to exercise over the administrators of the Poor Rate throughout the country.[33] Whatever powers the Board exercises beyond this limit were right and necessary in that peculiar case, for the cure of rooted habits of maladministration in matters deeply affecting not the localities merely, but the whole community; since no locality has a moral right to make itself by mismanagement a nest of pauperism, necessarily over-

33. The Poor Law Amendment Act of 1834 had established, as the central authority, a Poor Law Commission, consisting of three commissioners, not Members of Parliament, and responsible to the Home Secretary. In 1847 the Commission was replaced by a Poor Law Board, whose president or secretary was required to be a Member of Parliament and whose immediate responsibility was to Parliament.

flowing into other localities and impairing the moral and physical condition of the whole labouring community. The powers of administrative coercion and subordinate legislation possessed by the Poor Law Board (but which, owing to the state of opinion on the subject, are very scantily exercised by them), though perfectly justifiable in a case of first-rate national interest, would be wholly out of place in the superintendence of interests purely local. But a central organ of information and instruction for all the localities would be equally valuable in all departments of administration. A government cannot have too much of the kind of activity which does not impede, but aids and stimulates, individual exertion and development. The mischief begins when, instead of calling forth the activity and powers of individuals and bodies, it substitutes its own activity for theirs; when, instead of informing, advising, and, upon occasion, denouncing, it makes them work in fetters, or bids them stand aside and does their work instead of them. The worth of a State, in the long run, is the worth of the individuals composing it; and a State which postpones the interest of *their* mental expansion and elevation to a little more of administrative skill, or of that semblance of it which practice gives in the details of business; a State which dwarfs its men, in order that they may be more docile instruments in its hands even for beneficial purposes – will find that with small men no great thing can really be accomplished; and that the perfection of machinery to which it has sacrificed everything will in the end avail it nothing, for want of the vital power which, in order that the machine might work more smoothly, it has preferred to banish.

FOR THE BEST IN PAPERBACKS, LOOK FOR THE 🐧

In every corner of the world, on every subject under the sun, Penguin represents quality and variety – the very best in publishing today.

For complete information about books available from Penguin – including Pelicans, Puffins, Peregrines and Penguin Classics – and how to order them, write to us at the appropriate address below. Please note that for copyright reasons the selection of books varies from country to country.

In the United Kingdom: For a complete list of books available from Penguin in the U.K., please write to *Dept E.P., Penguin Books Ltd, Harmondsworth, Middlesex, UB7 0DA*

In the United States: For a complete list of books available from Penguin in the U.S., please write to *Dept BA, Penguin, 299 Murray Hill Parkway, East Rutherford, New Jersey 07073*

In Canada: For a complete list of books available from Penguin in Canada, please write to *Penguin Books Canada Ltd, 2801 John Street, Markham, Ontario L3R 1B4*

In Australia: For a complete list of books available from Penguin in Australia, please write to the *Marketing Department, Penguin Books Australia Ltd, P.O. Box 257, Ringwood, Victoria 3134*

In New Zealand: For a complete list of books available from Penguin in New Zealand, please write to the *Marketing Department, Penguin Books (NZ) Ltd, Private Bag, Takapuna, Auckland 9*

In India: For a complete list of books available from Penguin, please write to *Penguin Overseas Ltd, 706 Eros Apartments, 56 Nehru Place, New Delhi, 110019*

In Holland: For a complete list of books available from Penguin in Holland, please write to *Penguin Books Nederland B.V., Postbus 195, NL–1380AD Weesp, Netherlands*

In Germany: For a complete list of books available from Penguin, please write to *Penguin Books Ltd, Friedrichstrasse 10 – 12, D–6000 Frankfurt Main 1, Federal Republic of Germany*

In Spain: For a complete list of books available from Penguin in Spain, please write to *Longman Penguin España, Calle San Nicolas 15, E–28013 Madrid, Spain*

PENGUIN CLASSICS

Netochka Nezvanova   Fyodor Dostoyevsky

Dostoyevsky's first book tells the story of 'Nameless Nobody' and introduces many of the themes and issues which will dominate his great masterpieces.

Selections from the Carmina Burana   A verse translation by David Parlett

The famous songs from the *Carmina Burana* (made into an oratorio by Carl Orff) tell of lecherous monks and corrupt clerics, drinkers and gamblers, and the fleeting pleasures of youth.

Fear and Trembling   Søren Kierkegaard

A profound meditation on the nature of faith and submission to God's will which examines with startling originality the story of Abraham and Isaac.

Selected Prose   Charles Lamb

Lamb's famous essays (under the strange pseudonym of Elia) on anything and everything have long been celebrated for their apparently innocent charm; this major new edition allows readers to discover the darker and more interesting aspects of Lamb.

The Picture of Dorian Gray   Oscar Wilde

Wilde's superb and macabre novella, one of his supreme works, is reprinted here with a masterly Introduction and valuable Notes by Peter Ackroyd.

A Treatise of Human Nature   David Hume

A universally acknowledged masterpiece by 'the greatest of all British Philosophers' – A. J. Ayer

PENGUIN CLASSICS

A Passage to India   E. M. Forster

Centred on the unresolved mystery in the Marabar Caves, Forster's great work provides the definitive evocation of the British Raj.

The Republic   Plato

The best-known of Plato's dialogues, *The Republic* is also one of the supreme masterpieces of Western philosophy whose influence cannot be overestimated.

The Life of Johnson   James Boswell

Perhaps the finest 'life' ever written, Boswell's *Johnson* captures for all time one of the most colourful and talented figures in English literary history.

Remembrance of Things Past (3 volumes)   Marcel Proust

This revised version by Terence Kilmartin of C. K. Scott Moncrieff's original translation has been universally acclaimed – available for the first time in paperback.

Metamorphoses   Ovid

A golden treasury of myths and legends which has proved a major influence on Western literature.

A Nietzsche Reader   Friedrich Nietzsche

A superb selection from all the major works of one of the greatest thinkers and writers in world literature, translated into clear, modern English.

PENGUIN CLASSICS